EDITED AND WITH AN INTRODUCTION BY
RICHARD HOFSTADTER

E-70
F. C.

The Progressive Movement

1900–1915

PRENTICE-HALL, Inc., Englewood Cliffs, N.J.

Table of Contents

Introduction by Richard Hofstadter

Social and
Moral Issues

The Trusts and Big Business

The Meaning of
The Progressive Movement

*"We have been refreshed by a new insight into our own life. . . .
We have come now to the sober second thought. The scales of heed-
lessness have fallen from our eyes. We have made up our minds to
square every process of our national life again with the standards we
so proudly set up at the beginning and have always carried at our
hearts. Our work is a work of restoration." From Woodrow Wilson,*
Inaugural Address, *March 4, 1913.*

For a long time historians have written of the period roughly between
1900 and 1914 as the Progressive era, and of its variety of reform agita-
ions, as the Progressive movement. In these designations the historians
have followed the example of many of the period's leading figures, who
liked the ring of the word "Progressive" as applied to themselves. The
men of that age were proudly aware, even as they were fighting their
battles, that there was something distinctive about the political and social
life of their time which sharply marked it off from the preceding era of
materialism and corruption.

From the end of the Civil War to the close of the nineteenth century,
the physical energies of the American people had been mobilized for a
remarkable burst of material development, but their moral energies had
lain relatively dormant. Certain moral facets of the American character
had become all but invisible. It was as though the controversy over slavery, the Civil War itself, and the difficulties and failures of Reconstruction had exhausted the moral and political capacities of the people and
left them relieved to abandon crusades and reforms and to plunge instead
into the rewarding tasks of material achievement.

During this period American settlers and entrepreneurs had filled up
a vast area of land between the Mississippi River and California and had
spanned the country with a railroad network of more than a quarter of
a million miles. The number of farms, as well as the number of acres
under cultivation, had doubled between 1870 and 1900, and the production of wheat, cotton, and corn had increased from two to two-and-a-half
times.

Still more impressive was the growth of the urban and industrial seg-
ment of the economy. Whole systems of industry and whole regions of
industrial production were created. Between 1870 and 1900 the produc-

tion of bituminous coal increased five times, of crude petroleum twelve times, of steel ingots and castings more than 140 times. The urban population jumped from 9.9 million to 30.1 million, and thoughtful observers could see that the day was not very far off when the rural population would be outnumbered and the characteristic problems of the nation would be city problems. The larger cities grew at an almost alarming speed, and the pace of their growth seemed to outstrip their means of administration. Chicago, for example, more than doubled its population in the single decade 1880 to 1890, and a growth rate for that decade alone of from 60 to 80 per cent was not uncommon for the newer cities of the Middle West.

Toward the turn of the century it became increasingly evident that all this material growth had been achieved at a terrible cost in human value and in the waste of natural resources. The land and the people had both been plundered. The farmers, whose products had not only fed the expanding national working force but had also paid abroad for much of the foreign capital that financed American industrialization, had received pathetic returns for their toil. They had had little or no protection against exploitation by the railroads, against the high cost of credit, or against an unjust burden of taxation. At the same time the cities that grew with American industry were themselves industrial wastelands—centers of vice and poverty, ugly, full of crowded slums, badly administered. Industry after a period of hectic competition, was rapidly becoming concentrated a process which was hastened by the power of finance capital. Big business choked free competition and concentrated political power in a few hands. Stirred by such works as Ida Tarbell's account of the methods of the Standard Oil Company (Document 3), men began to realize how ruthless were the methods by which some great enterprises and great fortunes had been built, how business competitors and industrial workers alike had been exploited by the captains of industry. Moreover, business great and small, had debased politics: working with powerful bosses in city, state, and nation, it had won favors and privileges in return for its subsidies to corrupt machines. Domination of affairs by political bosses and business organizations was now seen to be a threat to democracy itself.

What had happened, as a great many men of good will saw it at the beginning of the Progressive era, was that in the extraordinary outburst of productive energy of the last few decades, the nation had not developed in any corresponding degree the means of meeting human needs or controlling or reforming the manifold evils that come with any such rapid physical change. The Progressive movement, then, may be looked upon as an attempt to develop the moral will, the intellectual insight and the political and administrative agencies to remedy the accumulated evils and negligences of a period of industrial growth. Since the Progressives were not revolutionists, it was also an attempt to work out a strategy for orderly social change.

Of course, not everyone looked at the evils that burdened society from quite the same point of view, and it would be a mistake to exaggerate the measure of agreement among those who were called, or chose to call themselves, Progressives. The larger their numbers, the more likely serious differences among them would be. And in a short time their numbers became large indeed. Perhaps the most remarkable thing about the Progressive movement was that it became so pervasive, that so many people could, at some time and on some issue, be called "Progressive." In the three-cornered presidential election of 1912, the two most popular candidates, Woodrow Wilson and Theodore Roosevelt, both ran on Progressive platforms and made Progressive-sounding speeches, and between them they had almost 70 per cent of the popular votes. Even the third candidate, President Taft, who had offended the Progressives in his own party and was inevitably cast in the conservative role, had been identified with some Progressive issues. Significantly, his party's leaders thought it wise to declare in their platform that they were "prepared to go forward with the solution of those new questions, which social, economic, and political development have brought to the forefront of the nation's interest," and to promise "to satisfy the just demand of the people for the study and solution of the complex and constantly changing problems of social welfare." Thus even the conservatism of 1912 thought it would be to its advantage to present itself as being, in some degree, "Progressive."

When a term becomes as widely adopted as this, we may justifiably be suspicious of the precision of its meaning. To speak of any two men of this era as being "Progressives" in their general political direction, does not mean that they will be in agreement on all social or political issues. One cannot forget the great heterogeneity of the country, or ignore the possibility that Progressivism could mean something different in the countryside from what it meant in the city, that it might have different principles in the Northeast as opposed to the South and West, that businessmen who favored some Progressive measures might have different hopes from those of professional and middle-class Progressives, and that Progressives in the farm country would have some special interests of their own.

It is necessary also to bear in mind the variety of issues about which one might or might not have taken a "Progressive" point of view: trusts and finance capital; bosses and popular control of politics; taxation and

tariffs; conservation; railroad rates and rebates; vice and corruption; the
conditions of labor and the role of labor unions; woman suffrage; the
rights of Negroes; referendum and recall; city reform; even Prohibition.
The diversity of these issues, and the diversity of social classes and social
interests that were at play in the political system, multiply the possibilities for disagreement within the Progressive movement. A businessman
and a labor leader might have common notions about a campaign against
corruption but have diametrically opposed ideas about the position of
trade unions. A small-town banker and a farmer might see eye-to-eye on
certain matters of financial reform, but have wholly different views on
the referendum and recall. Two harassed shippers might agree heartily
on the necessity of doing something about railroad rates but fall out over
tariff policy. No doubt there were at work in the Progressive movement
some persons who deserve the generic label of "reformers" for having
given enthusiastic support to most of the proposals for change that were
being agitated in their day. But there were also one-interest and one-
issue people, who worked arduously to advance this or that reform and
remained quite indifferent to the others.

Historians have rightly refused to allow such complications to prevent
them from speaking of the Progressive movement and the Progressive era.
It is the historian's business not only to take careful account of particulars
but also to assess the general direction of social movements in the past.
For all its internal differences and counter-currents, there were in Progressivism certain general tendencies, certain widespread commitments of
belief, which outweigh the particulars. It is these commitments and beliefs which make it possible to use the term "Progressive" in the hope
that the unity it conveys will not be misconstrued.

II

What were these distinguishing qualities that mark Progressivism? The
name itself may be slightly misleading here: of course, the Progressives
believed in progress; but so did a great many conservatives, who argued
that they had a sounder understanding of how progress works and of the
pace at which it goes on. The distinguishing thing about the Progressives
was something else, which for lack of a better term might be called "ac-
tivism": they argued that social evils will not remedy themselves, and
that it is wrong to sit by passively and wait for time to take care of them.
As Herbert Croly (Doc. 19) put it, they did not believe that the future
would take care of itself. They believed that the people of the country
should be stimulated to work energetically to bring about social progress,

that the positive powers of government must be used to achieve this end. Conservatives generally believed in time and nature to bring progress; Progressives believed in energy and governmental action.

The basic mood of Progressivism was intensely optimistic. One can, to be sure, find in the writings of some Progressives a note of anxiety (Doc. 1) as to what might happen to the country if various proposed reforms should fail to relieve the most threatening evils. Some of them feared that a continued concentration of power in the hands of investment banking firms—which they called "the money trust"—might in the long run undermine American democracy and the spirit of enterprise (Docs. 33, 34, 35). But the dominant note is one of confidence (Doc. 26), of faith that no problem is too difficult to be overcome by the proper mobilization of energy and intelligence in the citizenry. And when one thinks of the outstanding political leaders of the Progressive era—men like Theodore Roosevelt, Woodrow Wilson, William Jennings Bryan, and Robert M. La Follette—one thinks mainly of men with a certain faith, serene, militant, or buoyant, in the possibilities of the future. The movement was animated with the sense that something new and hopeful was being created —with a faith that found itself embodied in party slogans or the titles of important books: *The Old Order Changeth* (Docs. 21, 26), *The New Democracy* (Doc. 18), *The New Freedom* (Doc. 35), *The New Nationalism* (Doc. 24), *The Promise of American Life* (Doc. 19).

This promise of social progress was not to be realized by sitting and praying, but by using the active powers—by the exposure of evils through the spreading of information and the exhortation of the citizenry; by using the possibilities inherent in the ballot to find new and vigorous popular leaders; in short, by a revivification of democracy. As Walter Lippmann expressed it in the title of one of his early books (Doc. 36), the nation had finished with a policy of drift and was girding itself for the mastery of its own destiny. It was this that the "muckrakers" (Part I, especially Docs. 1, 2) thought gave special value to their voluminous and effective exposures of corruption, crime, waste, brutality, and autocracy in the dark corners of American life: they hoped that people would not read their sordid stories just for their shock value but that they would be filled with the desire to do something about corrupt bosses, sweated labor (Doc. 9), civic decay, monopolistic extortion. If the people were sufficiently aroused, they would wrest power away from city and state bosses (Doc. 21), millionaire senators (Doc. 22), and the other minions of invisible government and take it back into their own hands. Having done so, they would use their regained power—through the city, state, or federal governments, as the case might demand—to solve social and economic problems: tenements (Doc. 8) would be eliminated; the sweated labor of women and children (Docs. 5, 6, 17) would be forbidden; the Negro race (Doc. 7) would be supported in the struggle for its rights; extortionate tariffs (Docs. 31, 32) and monopoly prices would be regulated out of existence; social legislation (Docs. 9-12) would protect the working classes from the terrible hazards of industry; adulterated foods (Doc. 4) and falsely advertised drugs would be driven off the market; unfair competition by the great corporations (Doc. 3) would be subject to constant policing by government; the concentration of business control in the hands of a few powerful banking interests (Docs. 33, 34) would be broken up; better credit would be provided for farmers and small businessmen; the commercial exploitation of vice (Doc. 17) and drink would be reduced or eliminated.

III

Unlike the New Deal, which was a response to serious economic depression, Progressivism flourished during a period of comparative prosperity. Indeed, the Progressive movement was made possible only by a return of the prosperity after the depression of 1893-97. During that depression the fear of agricultural discontent, and the widespread conviction that the adoption of free coinage of silver would throw the country into economic chaos, caused the entire well-to-do middle class to stiffen its back against the dangers represented by the Populists and Bryanites. When those dangers were removed, the middle-class public felt free to relax, and then to express its own discontents and anxieties with the state of American society.

After 1897, as prosperity returned, there was a sharp upward turn in prices, which continued throughout the period. This up-turn, while it took some of the edge off the discontents of farmers, stimulated the discontents of many city dwellers. With the rising cost of living, many people, especially those living on more or less fixed incomes, became increasingly disturbed by charges that high tariffs (Doc. 31), business monopolies, inequitable taxation, civic graft, and indeed the activities of labor unions, were eating into their incomes. People became aware of their interests as consumers (Doc. 18), and accordingly gave their support to many Progressive demands.

At the same time, while rising prices relieved most farmers of the terrible pressures under which they had lived during the long deflationary period from 1869 to 1896, the farmers had not forgotten the old grievances against railroads, monopolies, bankers, and political bossism that had stimulated the Populist uprising of the 1890's and the Bryan campaign of 1896. Even now, under more bearable conditions, they were still likely to give their support to Progressive political leaders who promised them better regulation of railroad rates, tariff relief, better farm credits, and other economic gains. In this way, the reform sentiments of the country-side and the reform impulse of the city middle classes, which had previously worked independently of each other or at cross purposes, now came together in a common demand for certain types of legislation. Progressivism incorporated the heritage of Populism and Bryan Democracy.

While these two streams were coming together, a new kind of political leadership was emerging. Progressivism was largely the creation of a new and younger generation of politicians, who had come of age after the problems of Reconstruction had been largely settled, who had grown up along with post-Civil War industrialization, and who had never acquiesced in the crass and ruthless materialism of its captains of industry. These politicians were very often of well-established families, the sons of well-to-do professionals or business men, who were inspired by the high civic ideals kept alive since the Civil War by the Mugwump reformers. They saw that their own political careers were not to be made by catering to money makers, but by some more disinterested contribution either in the reform of industrial and political evils or in the promotion of America's interests in the arena of world politics—or, as in the case of Theodore Roosevelt, by both. Hence the Progressive movement was led by young men. In 1900 Robert M. La Follette was 45, Woodrow Wilson and Louis D. Brandeis were 44, Roosevelt 42, Bryan 40, Beveridge and Hughes 38, Borah 35, Hiram Johnson 34, Joseph W. Folk 31. The writers who did so much to shape the tone of the period were even younger; for Ida M. Tarbell was 43 in 1900, Herbert Croly 35, Lincoln Steffens 34, David Graham Phillips 33, Ray Stannard Baker 30, Walter Weyl 27, and Upton Sinclair only 22.

What politicians were doing in the field of public leadership, and what writers were doing in the field of reporting and exposure, a new generation of thinkers and scholars was doing in the academic world. Men like Charles A. Beard and J. Allen Smith in history and political science, Richard T. Ely, John R. Commons, and the acidulous Thorstein Veblen in economics, John Dewey in philosophy and education, Lester F. Ward, Edward A. Ross (Doc. 14), and Charles H. Cooley in sociology, and the admirers of Oliver Wendell Holmes, Jr., in jurisprudence (Doc. 10), were together developing a kind of social criticism that transcended the formalistic doctrines and methods of their predecessors and tried to cope with the sordid and often unacknowledged realities of the world. Men such as these were concerned not so much with formal political philosophies and the texts of constitutions as with the interests behind them, not so much with old-fashioned economic doctrine as with the actual development of economic institutions, not so much with the elaboration of philosophical or educational systems as with the progressive use of thought in action, not so much with the preaching of high social principles as with the development of detailed knowledge of the operation of social forces (Doc. 11), not so much with the elaboration of legal traditions as with the way in which legal decisions were actually arrived at. New political writers emerged, like Herbert Croly, the founder of the *New Republic* (Docs. 19, 27), and his colleagues Walter Lippmann (Doc. 36) and Walter Weyl (Doc. 18), who used the newer thought to analyze for a broad public the problems of the day, writing of the Progressives sometimes sympathetically and sometimes in a spirit of keen criticism.

Hardly less important than the work of academic and journalistic critics was the influence of social Christianity. For some time, large segments of the Protestant clergy had been alarmed at the violence of labor conflict, appalled at city living conditions, and troubled by the failure of the churches to win an adequate following among urban workers. During the 1890's the clerical conviction that Christianity, to make a contribution to solving the new moral problems of industrialism, must become a social force as well as a religious creed, had precipitated a strong movement to make the churches socially effective. The writings of such leaders of the social gospel as Washington Gladden and Walter Rauschenbush (Doc. 15) helped to give the Progressive movement the character of an evangelical revival in politics and economics. In the Progressive protest, the voice of the Christian conscience was heard more clearly than at any time since the days of the abolitionist movement.

Another notable feature of the era was the increasing role of women in American politics. Women had, of course, long been interested in reform movements, and had played a prominent part in abolitionism. But the numbers of women active in political affairs had been very limited. Now the educated, middle-class woman was beginning to grow tired of the passivity that was expected of her and sought to express herself in civic affairs. Her own interests as a mother were brought into play by her concern over the education and welfare of her children, the urban environment in which they lived, and such municipal facilities as playgrounds, schools, and parks. Her interests as a consumer were alerted by political struggles over tariffs, taxes, monopolies, and graft. But more important than her interests were her sympathies, for she was shocked by the revelations that were being made almost every day about the conditions of labor of women and children in the mills and mines of the country (Docs. 5, 6), of the conditions under which the urban poor lived in the tenement-house districts (Doc. 8). Women were beginning to develop their own heroes of philanthropic action, like Jane Addams (Doc. 17), the founder of the famous social settlement at Hull House in Chicago, and also to feel more strongly about their political rights. Believing that they were far better equipped than men to introduce into politics the note of morality and humane concern that the state of American society seemed to need so badly (Doc. 16), women in increasing numbers began to demand the vote for themselves. By 1914 they had the vote in eleven states, and their efforts were crowned with final success in the Nineteenth Amendment, which was ratified in 1920.

IV

If one examines the historical course of Progressive politics, one finds that the Progressive movement began in the cities, spread rapidly to the states, and reached the federal level most effectively in its later phases. Indeed, if one looks at the history of American cities, one is impressed with the fact that there Progressivism was really well under way in the 1890's, when the city governments of New York, Chicago, Detroit, Milwaukee, and others were reformed. By 1895 over seventy citizens' organizations had been formed to work for the improvement of city conditions.

But in law the cities were simply the creations of the states, and efforts to better municipal life forced reformers time and again to confront the power of the allies of local bosses who sat in the state legislatures. Moreover, many of the business abuses, from extortionate railroad rates to the exploitation of woman and child labor, were by their nature susceptible to reform only on the state level through statewide laws. Around the turn of the century, several of the reform leaders were elected state governors. Among the first of these was Robert M. La Follette (Docs. 23, 30), who was elected governor of Wisconsin in 1900, and who waged a courageous and moderately successful battle to regulate the railroads and public utilities of his state and tighten its tax system. Similar battles were fought in California by Hiram Johnson, in New York by Charles Evans Hughes, who had previously done notable work in exposing the corrupt practices of insurance companies, in Missouri by Joseph Folk, in Oregon by William S. U'Ren, and still later in New Jersey by Woodrow Wilson and in Ohio by James M. Cox.

In their struggles against railroads, utilities, insurance companies, and other business organizations, reformers were driven to do constant battle with the political machines fed by contributions from businessmen. They became convinced that in order to achieve lasting success, control of the political parties and the state and local governments must be taken out of the hands of venal bosses and put into the hands of the people. To this end, they proposed and succeeded in getting passed in many states democratic reforms of varying degrees of effectiveness (Doc. 26). Corrupt practices acts were intended to attack the illicit relation between money and politics. The direct primary was intended to put the choice of political candidates in the hands of the people, rather than the party machines, and thus raise the level of political leadership. The initiative made it possible for citizens' organizations to propose legislation, while the referendum made it possible for voters to pass on state laws. The short ballot was adopted to make it easier for the voter to perform his function intelligently. The recall of public officials was widely adopted as a means of removing corrupt or incompetent officials before the expiration of their terms of office. Finally, since many reform measures were being turned down by courts throughout the country, more advanced reformers began to advocate even the public recall of judges, and seven western states actually made provision for such recall. This proposal, which seemed to threaten the independence of the judiciary, was particularly shocking to conservatives, though the controversy it aroused was meaningless, since no judge of any superior or supreme court of any of the states having such laws was ever recalled. When Theodore Roosevelt, attempting to arrive at a compromise on the issue, suggested the recall of judicial *decisions* in 1912, he lost many of his Republican friends.

The demand for returning government to the people was carried from state government into national affairs. In the House of Representatives insurgents under the leadership of Champ Clark of Missouri and George W. Norris of Nebraska struck a blow at bossism when they took away from "Uncle Joe" Cannon, the Speaker, the power to control the workings of its vital Rules Committee. The Senate itself, which had long been stigmatized as a "millionaire's club" and a haunt of reactionary allies of big business (Doc. 22), was at last touched by the reform movement when the Seventeenth Amendment took the power to appoint Senators out of the hands of the legislatures and required direct election by the people.

In the sphere of social as well as political reform, much progress had already been made by state legislatures before 1900. By that year almost half the states had passed laws to limit the oppressive evil of child labor (Doc. 6), though much remained to be done. Many states, between 1896 and 1908, also attempted to limit the work-week for women. Often the conservative courts were disposed to regard laws governing the hours of

labor as violations of individual freedoms safeguarded by the Constitution; in one such case, a ruling of the Supreme Court brought forth
a stinging and memorable dissent from Justice Holmes (Doc. 10). But a
considerable gain for legislation protecting women was won in 1908, when
Louis D. Brandeis presented the Court with an unusual brief (Doc. 11),
more devoted to social realism than to legal argument, and persuaded
the Court to uphold an Oregon law limiting the working day for women
to ten hours (Doc. 12). In the following decade, 39 states either passed
new laws or fortified old laws dealing with the conditions of womens'
work. Many also passed laws setting minimum wage rates for women,
though these, again, were temporarily undermined by a Court decision
of 1923. Other important forms of social legislation were laws which
provided for accident insurance, and which gave aid to the aged poor
and to dependent children; mothers' assistance laws, intended to help
divorced, widowed, or deserted mothers, were passed. Laws aimed directly
at child labor were hard to enforce; but in most states, reformers also
got some results through raising the legal age at which children could
leave school.

V

Certain national problems, especially those involving big business, railroads, tariff, finance capital, and the like, were too large to be dealt with
effectively in the states. At the turn of the century it was already clear
that the demand for reform would reach national political leaders. When
the conservative McKinley was assassinated in 1901, his replacement by
a representative of the new generation, Theodore Roosevelt, only released
forces that were already in existence. Roosevelt himself was a combination
of moderate conservative and moderate Progressive, who did not believe
that trust-busting on a large scale was practicable or desirable (Doc. 28),
and who looked with some anxiety upon the discontent stirred up by
the muckrakers and other reformers (Doc. 2). But he was also opposed
to plutocratic arrogance, corruption, civic indifference, and materialism,
and he understood the need of right-thinking Americans to be reassured
about the ability of their government to cope with bosses, bankers, and
trusts. Although he did not act on a large scale against trusts, his prosecution of the Northern Securities Company (Doc. 29), one of the biggest
and best-known, established the point, as he said "that the most powerful
men in this country were held to accountability under the law." Again,
his settlement of the ominous anthracite strike of 1902, in the face of
arrogance and intransigent conduct by the mine owners, confirmed the

impression that the country at last had a President big enough to stand up to the great capitalist interests.

During Roosevelt's administration, Congress also set the basis for effective railroad regulation by passing the Hepburn Act, which, though it failed to satisfy the demands of ardent reformers like La Follette (Doc. 30), gave the Interstate Commerce Commission enough power to begin the substantial reduction of many rates. Congress responded to public pressures aroused by such muckrakers as Upton Sinclair (Doc. 4) and Samuel Hopkins Adams by enacting a Pure Food and Drug Act in 1906. A reform about which Roosevelt did have unbounded enthusiasm was the conservation of natural resources (Doc. 13), which had been squandered for generations. Roosevelt set aside millions of acres of timber and other lands as governmental reserves, put the zealous conservationist Gifford Pinchot in charge of the national forests, and in 1907 called a national conference of governors and others interested in conservation, which elevated the concern for conservation to a national movement.

Under William Howard Taft, Roosevelt's chosen successor, Progressivism seemed to be marking time, so far as the federal government was concerned. It was true that Taft pushed anti-trust activities far more vigorously than Roosevelt, and extended some conservation policies. But he failed ignominiously to win real tariff reform—an issue Roosevelt had entirely ducked—and his acceptance of the leadership of Senate conservatives offended Progressives. Increasingly, the insurgents within his own party struck off on their own. On a few issues they were successful. Not only did they break the power of "Uncle Joe" Cannon in the House, but they strengthened the power of the ICC with the Mann-Elkins Act and passed a Physical Evaluation Act, long sought by La Follette, which set up a more realistic framework for railroad regulation, based on the true value of railroad properties rather than on watered stock. They also pushed through (with some support from Taft) the Sixteenth Amendment, authorizing an income tax, which was ratified in 1913; and the Seventeenth Amendment, providing for popular election of Senators, was ratified the same year.

Taft's inability to command the loyalty of Progressives in his own party led to a Republican split, manifest in the insurgency of 1910, and finally in the formation of a new, though short-lived party, the Progressive party, whose 1912 platform (Doc. 25) may be taken almost as a consummatory statement of the social aims of the Progressive movement. The split in the Republican party between the followers of Theodore Roosevelt and those of Taft was a welcome opportunity to the Democrats, who had not elected a president since Cleveland in 1892. The forces of

Western and Southern agrarianism were still strong in the Democratic party; and Democratic Progressivism was somewhat more colored than that of the Republicans by old rural animosities. Like the Progressive party, the Democratic party endorsed a wide variety of reform proposals; but many Democrats considered Roosevelt's acceptance of bigness in business as a betrayal of what they felt to be the central goal in the Progressive movement—the restoration of a truly competitive business world. Woodrow Wilson's campaign speeches (Doc. 35) were a masterly restatement of this view; he argued that no government would be strong enough to regulate the interests satisfactorily if they were not broken up through antitrust action and the restoration of competition. In this way, the main argument between the two progressive-minded candidates in 1912 became an argument between regulated monopoly and regulated competition.

Backed by widespread Progressive sentiment in both parties, the Wilson administration set out vigorously to redeem its promises of business and tariff reform. In 1913, responding to an appeal by Wilson for real tariff reform (Doc. 31), Congress passed the Underwood Tariff, the first satisfactory downward revision since the Civil War. Its passage was probably made possible by an unprecedented act on Wilson's part: a bold appeal to the American public against the activities of business lobbyists, activities of the sort which had crippled all previous attempts at tariff revision (Doc. 32). Banking and credit reforms followed: with the creation of the Federal Reserve System in 1913 the United States devised, for the first time in its long history of unsatisfactory banking, a sound central banking system with adequate governmental direction. To make sure that farm credit facilities were adequate, Congress also passed the Federal Farm Loan Act in 1916 which enabled farmers to secure loans against farm lands and buildings, and the Warehouse Act, which made loans available against stored farm products.

To meet the demand for anti-trust legislation, the administration secured the passage of two laws in 1914. The first, the Federal Trade Commission Act, was intended to prevent unfair trade practices by creating a commission empowered to investigate corporations and to issue "cease and desist" orders when it found that such practices prevailed. Wilson's own appointees to this body, however, proved relatively lax, and in later years the Commission was frequently used as a way of encouraging business consolidation. The second law, the Clayton Act, was intended to expand the legal foundation for anti-trust action laid in the Sherman Act of 1890. A notable provision, demanded by A. F. of L. head Samuel Gompers (Doc. 20), seemed to exempt labor unions from prosecution as conspiracies in restraint of trade, but later decisions by the Court nulli-

fied its force. Since the Clayton Act was passed just on the eve of World
War I, however, it came into being just at a time when, in the interests
of wartime production, anti-trust activities were largely suspended.

VI

The Progressive movement was dependent upon the civic alertness and
the combative mood of a great part of the public. Such a mood cannot
last forever; perhaps what was most remarkable about the Progressives
was their ability to sustain reformist enthusiasm as long as they did. Even
the first World War, which in the end helped to destroy the Progressive
movement, was conducted with true Progressive fervor and under the
cover of Progressive thinking: for the war too became a crusade against
autocracy, an attempt to make the world safe for democracy. When the
reaction finally did come, it was sharp and decisive. The war left the
people fatigued with Wilsonian idealism and ready for a return to
"normalcy."

During the 1920's, as the public relaxed into a mood of acquiescence
in business domination, the transient character of much of Progressivism
became apparent. The Progressive movement had never succeeded in
remedying the maldistribution of wealth, which was increasing even as
its reforms were being passed. Now its very efforts to establish an apparatus for the effective regulation of business were constantly frustrated.
The Federal Trade Commission, for example, far from preventing unfair practices, as was intended, became an agency of business consolidation. The heroic efforts of the Progressives to uproot the bosses and put
government in the hands of the people also seemed to have failed, though
the Progressive legislation remained on the books as a possible check to
corrupt machines. The most durable aspect of Progressivism seems to
have been its social legislation; for even during the conservative 1920's
much of this legislation was extended, and in some states its enforcement
was improved.

Despite the transiency of many of its achievements, the heritage of the
Progressive movement cannot be considered small or unimportant. The
Progressives developed for the first time on a large scale a type of realistic
journalism and social criticism that has become a permanent quality of
American thinking. They gave renewed strength to a climate of opinion
hostile to monopoly and suspicious of arbitrary aggregates of business
power (Doc. 33), which forced big business to operate circumspectly and
even to exercise some self-restraint. The traditions of responsible government and forceful leadership exemplified by men like Theodore Roose-

elt and Woodrow Wilson established unforgettable high points in American statesmanship. Finally, the reforms of the Progressive era established a basis and a precedent for further reforms to be passed when the need for them was felt. Franklin D. Roosevelt's New Deal owed a heavy debt to its Progressive forerunners both for moral inspiration and for some of its administrative devices.

The men and women of the Progressive movement must be considered, in this regard, to be pioneers of the welfare state. This was not because they sought to foster big government for its own sake. But they were determined to remedy the most pressing and dangerous social ills of industrial society, and in the attempt they quickly learned that they could not achieve their ends without using the power of the administrative state. Moreover, they asserted—and they were the first in our history to do so with real practical success—the idea that government cannot be viewed merely as a cold and negative policing agency, but that it has a wide and pervasive responsibility for the welfare of its citizens, and for the poor and powerless among them. For this, Progressivism must be understood as a major episode in the history of the American conscience.

PART ONE

The Muckrakers

DOCUMENT ONE

S. S. McClure Discovers
A Trend of the Times

January, 1903

Early in 1903, S. S. McClure, editor and publisher of the successful popular magazine, McClure's, *looked at his magazine and discovered an unplanned convergence among three of his articles, all of which revealed, as he saw it, a pervasive contempt for law. In calling attention to the significance of these three articles, all by writers who were to become famous as muckrakers, McClure marked the first self-awareness of muckraking as a social and journalistic movement. But he also gave expression to a statement of some characteristic concerns of the Progressive movement.* McClure's, January, 1903.

CONCERNING THREE ARTICLES IN THIS NUMBER OF MC CLURE'S,
AND A COINCIDENCE THAT MAY SET US THINKING

How many of those who have read through this number of the magazine noticed that it contains three articles on one subject? We did not plan it so; it is a coincidence that the January *McClure's* is such an arraignment of American character as should make every one of us stop and think. How many noticed that?

The leading article, "The Shame of Minneapolis," might have been called "The American Contempt of Law." That title could well have served for the current chapter of Miss Tarbell's History of Standard Oil. And it would have fitted perfectly Mr. Baker's "The Right to Work." All together, these articles come pretty near showing how universal is this dangerous trait of ours.

Miss Tarbell has our capitalists conspiring among themselves, deliberately, shrewdly, upon legal advice, to break the law so far as it restrained them, and to misuse it to restrain others who were in their way. Mr. Baker shows labor, the ancient enemy of capital, and the chief complainant of the trusts' unlawful acts, itself committing and excusing crimes. And in "The Shame of Minneapolis" we see the administration of a city employing criminals to commit crimes for the profit of the elected officials, while the citizens—Americans of good stock and more than average culture, and honest, healthy Scandinavians—stood by complacent and not alarmed.

Capitalists, workingmen, politicians, citizens—all breaking the law, or letting it be broken. Who is left to uphold it? The lawyers? Some of the best lawyers in this country are hired, not to go into court to defend cases, but to advise corporations and business firms how they can get around the law without too great a risk of punishment. The judges? Too many of them so respect the laws that for some "error" or quibble they restore to office and liberty men convicted on evidence overwhelmingly convincing to common sense. The churches? We know of one, an ancient and wealthy establishment, which had to be compelled by a Tammany hold-over health officer to put its tenements in sanitary condition. The colleges? They do not understand.

There is no one left; none but all of us. Capital is learning (with indignation at labor's unlawful acts) that its rival's contempt of law is a menace to property. Labor has shrieked the belief that the illegal power of capital is a menace to the worker. These two are drawing together. Last November when a strike was threatened by the yard-men on all the railroads centering in Chicago, the men got together and settled by raising wages, and raising freight rates too. They made the public pay. We all are doing our worst and making the public pay. The public is the people. We forget that we all are the people; that while each of us in his group can shove off on the rest the bill of today, the debt is only postponed; the rest are passing it on back to us. We have to pay in the end, every one of us. And in the end the sum total of the debt will be our liberty.

Theodore Roosevelt Finds
A Name for the Muckrakers

April 14, 1906

*President Roosevelt had mixed feelings about the value of the litera-
ture of exposure, which, by 1906, was beginning to flood the nation.
On one hand, he believed in warring on evil practices, but on the
other he was afraid that the new journalism was building up a
"revolutionary feeling" in the public that might become dangerous.
In the speech excerpted here, delivered at the laying of the corner-
stone of the House Office Building, he not only gave the muckrakers
the name that has gone down in history but also warned against the
possible excesses of their activities.* Presidential Addresses and State
Papers (*New York, 1910*), *vol. V, pp. 712-15.*

. . . In Bunyan's "Pilgrim's Progress" you may recall the description
of the Man with the Muck-rake, the man who could look no way but
downward, with the muck-rake in his hand; who was offered a celestial
crown for his muck-rake, but who would neither look up nor regard the
crown he was offered, but continued to rake to himself the filth of the
floor.

In "Pilgrim's Progress" the Man with the Muck-rake is set forth as the
example of him whose vision is fixed on carnal instead of on spiritual
things. Yet he also typifies the man who in this life consistently refuses
to see aught that is lofty, and fixes his eyes with solemn intentness only
on that which is vile and debasing. Now, it is very necessary that we
should not flinch from seeing what is vile and debasing. There is filth
on the floor, and it must be scraped up with the muck-rake; and there
are times and places where this service is the most needed of all the
services that can be performed. But the man who never does anything
else, who never thinks or speaks or writes, save of his feats with the muck-
rake, speedily becomes, not a help to society, not an incitement to good,
but one of the most potent forces for evil.

There are, in the body politic, economic and social, many and grave
evils, and there is urgent necessity for the sternest war upon them. There
should be relentless exposure of and attack upon every evil man whether
politician or business man, every evil practice, whether in politics, in
business, or in social life. I hail as a benefactor every writer or speaker,
every man who, on the platform, or in book, magazine, or newspaper,

with merciless severity makes such attack, provided always that he in his
turn remembers that the attack is of use only if it is absolutely truthful.
The liar is no whit better than the thief, and if his mendacity takes the
form of slander, he may be worse than most thieves. It puts a premium
upon knavery untruthfully to attack an honest man, or even with hysteri-
cal exaggeration to assail a bad man with untruth. An epidemic of indiscriminate assault upon character does not good, but very great harm.
The soul of every scoundrel is gladdened whenever an honest man is
assailed, or even when a scoundrel is untruthfully assailed.

Now, it is easy to twist out of shape what I have just said, easy to
affect to misunderstand it, and, if it is slurred over in repetition, not
difficult really to misunderstand it. Some persons are sincerely incapable
of understanding that to denounce mud slinging does not mean the in-
dorsement of whitewashing; and both the interested individuals who need
whitewashing, and those others who practice mud slinging, like to encourage such confusion of ideas. One of the chief counts against those
who make indiscriminate assault upon men in business or men in public
life, is that they invite a reaction which is sure to tell powerfully in favor
of the unscrupulous scoundrel who really ought to be attacked, who
ought to be exposed, who ought, if possible, to be put in the penitentiary.
If Aristides is praised overmuch as just, people get tired of hearing it;
and overcensure of the unjust finally and from similar reasons results in
their favor.

Any excess is almost sure to invite a reaction; and, unfortunately, the
reaction, instead of taking the form of punishment of those guilty of the
excess, is very apt to take the form either of punishment of the unoffend-
ing or of giving immunity, and even strength, to offenders. The effort to
make financial or political profit out of the destruction of character can
only result in public calamity. Gross and reckless assaults on character,
whether on the stump or in newspaper, magazine, or book, create a mor-
bid and vicious public sentiment, and at the same time act as a profound
deterrent to able men of normal sensitiveness and tend to prevent them
from entering the public service at any price. . . .

At the risk of repetition let me say again that my plea is, not for immunity to but for the most unsparing exposure of the politician who
betrays his trust, of the big business man who makes or spends his fortune in illegitimate or corrupt ways. There should be a resolute effort to
hunt every such man out of the position he has disgraced. Expose the
crime, and hunt down the criminal; but remember that even in the case
of crime, if it is attacked in sensational, lurid, and untruthful fashion,
the attack may do more damage to the public mind than the crime
itself. . . .

Ida M. Tarbell on the Methods of The Standard Oil Company

December, 1902

Ida M. Tarbell, who had already written popular works on Lincoln and Napoleon, was commissioned by S. S. McClure not to do a work of exposure but to tell the story of the remarkable achievements of Standard Oil. However, Miss Tarbell had lived among the independent oil operators of Pennsylvania and looked at this gigantic company through the eyes of its defeated competitors. Her account became the story of the ruthless methods by which this company was built, and it was so effective in blackening the name of John D. Rockefeller that he found it wise to hire a publicity agent to create a more favorable image of himself in the public mind. McClure's, December, 1902.

In the fall of 1871, while Mr. Rockefeller and his friends were occupied with all these questions certain Pennsylvania refiners, it is not too certain who, brought to them a remarkable scheme, the gist of which was to bring together secretly a large enough body of refiners and shippers to compel all the railroads handling oil to give to the company formed special rebates on its oil, and drawbacks on that of others. If they could get such rates, it was evident that those outside of their combination could not compete with them long, and that they would become eventually the only refiners. They could then limit their output to actual demand, and so keep up prices. This done, they could easily persuade the railroads to transport no crude for exportation, so that the foreigners would be forced to buy American refined. They believed that the price of oil thus exported could easily be advanced 50 per cent. The control of the refining interests would also enable them to fix their own price on crude. As they would be the only buyers and sellers, the speculative character of the business would be done away with. In short, the scheme they worked out put the entire oil business in their hands. It looked as simple to put into operation as it was dazzling in its results. . . .

The first thing was to get a charter—quietly. At a meeting held in Philadelphia late in the fall of 1871, a friend of one of the gentlemen interested mentioned to him that a certain estate then in liquidation had a charter for sale which gave its owners the right to carry on any kind of business in any country and in any way; that it could be bought for what it would cost to get a charter under the general laws of the state, and it would be a favor to the heirs to buy it. The opportunity was promptly taken. The name of the charter bought was the "Southern [usually written South] Improvement Company." For a beginning it was as good a name as another, since it said nothing.

With this charter in hand Mr. Rockefeller and Mr. Watson and their associates began to seek converts. In order that their great scheme might not be injured by premature public discussion, they asked of each person whom they approached a pledge of secrecy. Two forms of the pledges required before anything was revealed were published later. The first of these, which appeared in the New York *Tribune,* read as follows:

> I, A.B., do faithfully promise upon my honor and faith as a gentleman, that I will keep secret all transactions which I may have with the corporation known as the South Improvement Company; that, should I fail to complete any bargains with the said company, all the preliminary conversations shall be kept strictly private; and, finally, that I will not disclose the price for which I dispose of my product, or any other facts which may in any way bring to light the internal workings or organization of the company. All this I do freely promise.
>
> ....Signed. . . .

That they met with encouragement is evident from the fact that, when the corporators came together on January 2, 1872, in Philadelphia, for the first time under their charter, and transferred the company to the stockholders, they represented in one way or another a large part of the refining interest of the country. At this meeting 1,100 shares of the stock of the company, which was divided into 2,000 shares of $100 each, were subscribed for, and 20 per cent of their value paid in. Just who took stock at this meeting the writer has not been able to discover. At the same time, a discussion came up as to what refiners were to be allowed to go into the new company. Each of the men represented had friends whom he wanted taken care of, and after considerable discussion it was decided to take in every refinery they could get hold of. This decision was largely due to the railroad men. Mr. Watson had seen them as soon as the plans for the company were formed, and they had all agreed that if they gave rebates all refineries then existing must be taken in.

Very soon after this meeting of January 2 the rest of the stock of the South Improvement Company was taken. The complete list of stockholders, with their holdings, was as follows:

William Frew, Philadelphia, Pa. .... 10 shares
W. P. Logan, Philadelphia, Pa. .... 10 "
John P. Logan, Philadelphia, Pa. .... 10 "
Chas. Lockhart, Pittsburgh, Pa. .... 10 "
Richard S. Waring, Pittsburgh, Pa. .... 10 "
W. G. Warden, Philadelphia, Pa. .... 475 "
O. F. Waring, Pittsburgh, Pa. .... 475 "
P. H. Watson, Ashtabula, Ohio .... 100 "
H. M. Flagler, Cleveland, Ohio .... 180 "
O. H. Payne, Cleveland, Ohio .... 180 "
Wm. Rockefeller, Cleveland, Ohio .... 180 "
J. A. Bostwick, New York, N. Y. .... 180 "
John D. Rockefeller, Cleveland, Ohio .... 180 "
                                                         ‾‾‾‾‾
                                                         2,000 "

Mr. Watson was elected president and Mr. Warden secretary of the new association. It will be noticed that the largest individual holdings in the company were those of W. G. Warden, of Philadelphia, and O. F. Waring, of Pittsburgh, each of whom had 475 shares. The company most heavily interested in the South Improvement Company was the Standard Oil Company of Cleveland, Messrs. J. D. Rockefeller, William Rockefeller, O. H. Payne, and H. M. Flagler, all stockholders of that company, each having 180 shares—720 in the company.

The organization complete, there remained contracts to be made with the railroads. Three systems were interested: the Central, which, by its connection with the Lake Shore and Michigan Southern, ran directly into the Oil Regions; the Erie, allied with the Atlantic and Great Western, with a short line likewise tapping the heart of the region; and the Pennsylvania, with the connections known as the Allegheny Valley and Oil Creek Railroad. The persons to be won over were W. H. Vanderbilt, of the Central; W. H. Clarke, president of the Lake Shore and Michigan Southern; Jay Gould, of the Erie; General G. B. McClellan, president of the Atlantic and Great Western; and Tom Scott, of the Pennsylvania. There seems to have been little difficulty in persuading any of these persons to go into the scheme. It was, of course, a direct violation of their charters as public carriers, but such violations had been in practice for at least four years in the oil business, and for a longer period in other industries. Under pressure or persuasion all of these roads granted special rates. For years they had been fighting bitterly for the oil trade, often cutting rates to get a consignment, until there was no profit in it. They were glad enough to go into any arrangement which guaranteed each a sure percentage of the business and

gave them a profit on it. This the South Improvement Company did.
They seem not to have agreed to the contracts until the company assured them that all the refiners were going in. The contracts they made
were not on condition, however, that all were included. Three months
after they were signed Congress investigated the great scheme. The
testimony of the secretary of the company on this point before the
Congressional committee is worth reading:

Q. You say you made propositions to railroad companies, which they agreed to
accept upon the condition that you could include all the refineries?

A. No, sir; I did not say that; I said that was the understanding when we discussed this matter with them; it was no proposition on our part; they discussed it, not in the form of a proposition that the refineries should be all
taken in, but it was the intention and resolution of the company from the
first that that should be the result; we never had any other purpose in the
matter.

Q. In case you could take the refineries all in, the railroads proposed to give
you a rebate upon their freight charges?

A. No, sir; it was not put in that form; we were to put the refineries all in
upon the same terms; it was the understanding with the railroad companies
that we were to have a rebate; there was no rebate given in consideration of
our putting the companies all in, but we told them we would do it; the contract with the railroad companies was with us.

Q. But if you did form a company composed of the proprietors of all these refineries, you were to have a rebate upon your freight charges?

A. No; we were to have a rebate anyhow, but were to give all the refineries the
privilege of coming in.

Q. You were to have the rebate whether they came in or not?

A. Yes, sir.

"What effect were these arrangements to have upon those who did
not come into the combination?" asked the chairman.

"I do not think we ever took that question up," answered Mr. Warden.

A second objection to making a contract with the company came
from Mr. Scott, of the Pennsylvania road. "You take no account here,"
Mr. Scott told the secretary, W. G. Warden, who discussed the matter
at length with him, "of the oil producer—the man to whom the world
owes the business. You can never succeed unless you take care of the
producer." Mr. Warden objected strongly to forming a combination
with them. "The interests of the producers were in one sense antagonistic to ours; one as the seller and the other as the buyer. We held in
argument that the producers were abundantly able to take care of their
own branch of the business if they took care of the quantity produced."

So strongly did Mr. Scott argue, however, that finally the members of the South Improvement Company yielded, and a draft of an agreement, to be proposed to the producers, was drawn up in lead pencil; it was never presented. It seems to have been used principally to quiet Mr. Scott.

The work of persuasion went on swiftly. By the eighteenth of January the president of the Pennsylvania road, J. Edgar Thompson, had put his signature to the contract, and soon after Mr. Vanderbilt and Mr. Clarke signed for the Central system, and Jay Gould and General McClellan for the Erie. The contracts to which these gentlemen put their names fixed gross rates of freight from all common points, as the leading shipping points within the Oil Regions were called, to all the great refining and shipping centers—New York, Philadelphia, Baltimore, Pittsburgh and Cleveland. For example, the open rate on crude oil to New York was put at $2.56. On this price the South Improvement Company was allowed a rebate of $1.06 for its shipments; but it got not only this rebate, it was given in cash a like amount on each barrel of crude shipped by parties outside the combination.

The open rate from Cleveland to New York was $2.00, and 50 cents of this sum was turned over to the South Improvement Company, which at the same time received a rebate enabling it to ship for $1.50. Again an independent refiner in Cleveland paid 80 cents a barrel to get his crude from the Oil Regions to his works, and the railroad sent 40 cents of this money to the South Improvement Company. At the same time it cost the Cleveland refiner in the combination but 40 cents to get his crude oil. Like drawbacks and rebates were given for all points —Pittsburgh, Philadelphia, Boston and Baltimore.

An interesting provision in the contracts was that full waybills of all petroleum shipped over the roads should each day be sent to the South Improvement Company. This, of course, gave them knowledge of just who was doing business outside of their company—of how much business he was doing, and with whom he was doing it. Not only were they to have full knowledge of the business of all shippers—they were to have access to all books of the railroads. . . .

The reason given by the railroads in the contract for granting these extraordinary privileges was that the "magnitude and extent of the business and operations" purposed to be carried on by the South Improvement Company would greatly promote the interest of the railroads and make it desirable for them to encourage their undertaking. The evident advantages received by the railroad were a regular amount of freight—the Pennsylvania was to have 45 per cent of the eastbound

hipping, the Erie and Central each 27½ per cent, while westbound
reight was to be divided equally between them—fixed rates, and free-
om from the system of cutting which they had all found so harassing
nd disastrous.

It was on the second of January 1872 that the organization of the
outh Improvement Company was completed. The day before, the Stand-
rd Oil Company of Cleveland increased its capital from $1,000,000 to
2,500,000, "all the stockholders of the company being present and vot-
1g therefor." . . . The last three were officers and stockholders in
1e or more of the railroads centering in Cleveland. Three weeks after
1is increase of capital Mr. Rockefeller had the charter and contracts
f the South Improvement Company in hand, and was ready to see
·hat they would do in helping him carry out his idea of wholesale
ombination in Cleveland. There were at that time some twenty-six
efineries in the town—some of them very large plants. All of them were
·eling more or less the discouraging effects of the last three or four
ears of railroad discriminations in favor of the Standard Oil Company.
·o the owners of these refineries Mr. Rockefeller now went one by one,
nd explained the South Improvement Company. "You see," he told
1em, "this scheme is bound to work. It means an absolute control by
s of the oil business. There is no chance for anyone outside. But we
·e going to give everybody a chance to come in. You are to turn over
our refinery to my appraisers, and I will give you Standard Oil Com-
any stock or cash, as you prefer, for the value we put upon it. I advise
ou to take the stock. It will be for your good." Certain refiners ob-
·cted. They did not want to sell. They did want to keep and manage
1eir business. Mr. Rockefeller was regretful, but firm. It was useless to
·sist, he told the hesitating; they would certainly be crushed if they
id not accept his offer, and he pointed out in detail, and with gentle-
·ess, how beneficent the scheme really was—preventing the Creek re-
ners from destroying Cleveland, keeping up the price of refined oil,
estroying competition, and eliminating speculation.

The perfection of the scheme, the inevitableness of the result, the
·ersuasiveness of its advocate, the promise of great profits were different
·asons for leading many of the refiners to succumb at once. Some of
1em took stock—more took money.

A few of the refiners contested before surrendering. Among these was
.obert Hanna, an uncle of Mark Hanna, of the firm of Hanna, Basling-
·n & Co. Mr. Hanna had been refining oil since July 1869. According
· his own sworn statement he had made money, fully 60 per cent on
is investment the first year, and after that 30 per cent. Some time in

February 1872 the Standard Oil Company asked an interview with hi
and his associates. They wanted to buy his works, they said. "But
don't want to sell," objected Mr. Hanna. "You can never make a
more money, in my judgment," said Mr. Rockefeller. "You can't co
pete with the Standard. We have all the large refineries now. If y
refuse to sell, it will end in your being crushed." Hanna and Baslingt
were not satisfied. They went to see Mr. Watson, president of t
South Improvement Company, and an officer of the Lake Shore, ar
General Devereux, manager of the Lake Shore road. They were to
that the Standard had special rates; that it was useless to try to co
pete with them. General Devereux explained to the gentlemen that t
privileges granted the Standard were the legitimate and necessary a
vantage of the large shipper over the smaller, and that if Hanna, B
lington & Co. could give the road as large a quantity of oil as t
Standard did, with the same regularity, they could have the same rat
General Devereux says they "recognized the propriety" of his excus
They certainly recognized its authority. They say that they were sat
fied they could no longer get rates to and from Cleveland which wou
enable them to live, and "reluctantly" sold out. It must have been
luctantly, for they had paid $75,000 for their works, and had made
per cent a year on an average on their investment, and the Standa
appraiser allowed them $45,000. "Truly and really less than one-half
what they were absolutely worth, with a fair and honest competitio
in the lines of transportation," said Mr. Hanna, eight years later, in
affidavit.

Under the combined threat and persuasion of the Standard, arm
with the South Improvement Company scheme, almost the entire ind
pendent oil interest of Cleveland collapsed in three months' time. (
the twenty-six refineries, at least twenty-one sold out. From a capaci
of probably not over 1,500 barrels of crude a day, the Standard O
Company rose in three months' time to one of 10,000 barrels. By th
maneuver it became master of over one-fifth of the refining capaci
of the United States. Its next individual competitior was Sloan & Fle
ing, of New York, whose capacity was 1,700 barrels. The Standard h
a greater capacity than the entire Oil Creek Regions, greater than t
combined New York refiners. The transaction by which it acquired th
power was so stealthy that not even the best-informed newspaperme
of Cleveland knew what went on. It had all been accomplished in a
cordance with one of Mr. Rockefeller's chief business principles—"$
lence is golden."

While Mr. Rockefeller was working out the "good of the oil busines in Cleveland, his associates were busy at other points. A little more time and the great scheme would be an accomplished fact. And then there fell in its path two of those never-to-be-foreseen human elements which so often block great maneuvers. The first was born of a man's anger. The man had learned of the scheme. He wanted to go into it, but the directors were suspicious of him. He had been concerned in speculative enterprises and in dealings with the Erie road which had injured these directors in other days. They didn't want him to have any of the advantages of their great enterprise. When convinced that he could not share in the deal, he took his revenge by telling people in the Oil Regions what was going on. At first the Oil Regions refused to believe, but in a few days another slip born of human weakness came in to prove the rumor true. The schedule of rates agreed upon by the South Improvement Company and the railroads had been sent to the freight agent of the Lake Shore Railroad, but no order had been given to put them in force. The freight agent had a son on his death-bed. Distracted by his sorrow, he left his office in charge of subordinates, but neglected to tell them that the new schedules on his desk were a secret compact, whose effectiveness depended upon their being held until all was complete. On February 26 the subordinates, ignorant of the nature of the rates, put them in effect. The independent oil men heard with amazement that freight rates had been put up nearly 100 per cent. They needed no other proof of the truth of the rumors of conspiracy which were circulating. . . .

Upton Sinclair on
The Chicago Stockyards
1906

As a Socialist, Upton Sinclair wrote his novel The Jungle *to awaken sympathy for the plight of the workers in the Chicago slaughtering industry by portraying the life of an immigrant worker and his family. But his book's great impact came largely from its graphic and sometimes nauseating account of the conditions of slaughtering. It contributed a great deal to the pressure for the Pure Food and Drug Act, which was passed in the year it appeared.* The Jungle *(New York, 1906), pp. 114-17, 160-62.*

. . . It seemed as if every time you met a person from a new department, you heard of new swindles and new crimes. There was, for instance, a Lithuanian who was a cattle butcher for the plant where Marija had worked, which killed meat for canning only; and to hear this man describe the animals which came to his place would have been worth while for a Dante or a Zola. It seemed that they must have agencies all over the country, to hunt out old and crippled and diseased cattle to be canned. There were cattle which had been fed on "whisky-malt," the refuse of the breweries, and had become what the men called "steerly"—which means covered with boils. It was a nasty job killing these, for when you plunged your knife into them they would burst and splash foul-smelling stuff into your face; and when a man's sleeves were smeared with blood, and his hands steeped in it, how was he ever to wipe his face, or to clear his eyes so that he could see? It was stuff such as this that made the "embalmed beef" that had killed several times as many United States soldiers as all the bullets of the Spaniards; only the army beef, besides, was not fresh canned, it was old stuff that had been lying for years in the cellars.

Then one Sunday evening, Jurgis sat puffing his pipe by the kitchen stove, and talking with an old fellow whom Jonas had introduced, and who worked in the canning rooms at Durham's; and so Jurgis learned a few things about the great and only Durham canned goods, which had become a national institution. They were regular alchemists at Durham's; they advertised a mushroom-catsup, and the men who made it did not know what a mushroom looked like. They advertised "potted chicken,"—and it was like the boardinghouse soup of the comic papers, through which a chicken had walked with rubbers on. Perhaps they had a secret process for making chickens chemically—who knows? said Jurgis' friend; the things that went into the mixture were tripe, and the fat of pork, and beef suet, and hearts of beef, and finally the waste ends of veal, when they had any. They put these up in several grades, and sold them at several prices; but the contents of the cans all came out of the same hopper. And then there was "potted game" and "potted grouse," "potted ham," and "deviled ham"—de-vyled, as the men called it. "De-vyled" ham was made out of the waste ends of smoked beef that were too small to be sliced by the machines; and also tripe, dyed with chemicals so that it would not show white; and trimmings of hams and corned beef; and potatoes, skins and all; and finally the hard cartilaginous gullets of beef, after the tongues had been cut out. All this ingenious mixture was ground up and flavored with spices to make it taste like something. Anybody who could invent a new imitation had been sure of a fortune from old Durham, said Jurgis' informant; but it was hard to think of anything new in a place where so many sharp wits had been at work for so long; where men welcomed tuberculosis in the cattle they were feeding, because it made them fatten more quickly; and where they bought up all the old rancid butter left over in the grocery stores of a continent, and "oxidized" it by a forced-air process, to take away the odor, rechurned it with skim milk, and sold it in bricks in the cities! Up to a year or two ago it had been the custom to kill horses in the yards—ostensibly for fertilizer; but after long agitation the newspapers had been able to make the public realize that the horses were being canned. Now it was against the law to kill horses in Packingtown, and the law was really complied with—for the present, at any rate. Any day, however, one might see sharp-horned and shaggy-haired creatures running with the sheep—and yet what a job you would have to get the public to believe that a good part of what it buys for lamb and mutton is really goat's flesh!

There was another interesting set of statistics that a person might have gathered in Packingtown—those of the various afflictions of the workers. When Jurgis had first inspected the packing plants with Szedvilas, he had marveled while he listened to the tale of all the things that were made out of the carcasses of animals, and of all the lesser industries that were maintained there; now he found that each one of these lesser industries was a separate little inferno, in its way as horrible as the killing beds, the source and fountain of them all. The workers in each of them had their own peculiar diseases. And the wandering visitor might be skeptical about all the swindles, but he could

not be skeptical about these, for the worker bore the evidence of them
about on his own person—generally he had only to hold out his hand

There were the men in the pickle rooms, for instance, where ol
Antanas had gotten his death; scarce a one of these that had not som
spot of horror on his person. Let a man so much as scrape his finge
pushing a truck in the pickle rooms, and he might have a sore tha
would put him out of the world; all the joints in his fingers might b
eaten by the acid, one by one. Of the butchers and floorsmen, th
beef-boners and trimmers, and all those who used knives, you coul
scarcely find a person who had the use of his thumb; time and tim
again the base of it had been slashed, till it was a mere lump of fles
against which the man pressed the knife to hold it. The hands c
these men would be criss-crossed with cuts, until you could no longe
pretend to count them or to trace them. They would have no nails,-
they had worn them off pulling hides; their knuckles were swolle
so that their fingers spread out like a fan. There were men who worke
in the cooking rooms, in the midst of steam and sickening odors, b
artificial light; in these rooms the germs of tuberculosis might live fc
two years, but the supply was renewed every hour. There were the bee
luggers, who carried two-hundred-pound quarters into the refrigerato
cars; a fearful kind of work, that began at four o'clock in the mornin,
and that wore out the most powerful men in a few years. There wen
those who worked in the chilling rooms, and whose special disease wa
rheumatism; the time limit that a man could work in the chilling roon
was said to be five years. There were the wool-pluckers, whose hanc
went to pieces even sooner than the hands of the pickle men; for th
pelts of the sheep had to be painted with acid to loosen the wool, an
then the pluckers had to pull out this wool with their bare hands, ti
the acid had eaten their fingers off. There were those who made the tin
for the canned meat; and their hands, too, were a maze of cuts, an
each cut represented a chance for blood poisoning. Some worked at th
stamping machines, and it was very seldom that one could work lon
there at the pace that was set, and not give out and forget himsel
and have a part of his hand chopped off. There were the "hoisters,
as they were called, whose task it was to press the lever which lifte
the dead cattle off the floor. They ran along upon a rafter, peerin
down through the damp and the steam; and as old Durham's architec
had not built the killing room for the convenience of the hoisters, a
every few feet they would have to stoop under a beam, say four fee
above the one they ran on; which got them into the habit of stoopin,

o that in a few years they would be walking like chimpanzees. Worst
f any, however, were the fertilizer men, and those who served in the
ooking rooms. These people could not be shown to the visitor,—for
he odor of a fertilizer man would scare any ordinary visitor at a hundred yards, and as for the other men, who worked in tank rooms full
f steam, and in some of which there were open vats near the level of
he floor, their peculiar trouble was that they fell into the vats; and
when they were fished out, there was never enough of them left to be
worth exhibiting,—sometimes they would be overlooked for days, till all
but the bones of them had gone out to the world as Durham's Pure
Leaf Lard! . . .

With one member trimming beef in a cannery, and another work-
ng in a sausage factory, the family had a first-hand knowledge of the
reat majority of Packingtown swindles. For it was the custom, as they
ound, whenever meat was so spoiled that it could not be used for any-
hing else, either to can it or else to chop it up into sausage. With
what had been told them by Jonas, who had worked in the pickle rooms,
hey could now study the whole of the spoiled-meat industry on the in-
ide, and read a new and grim meaning into that old Packingtown jest
—that they use everything of the pig except the squeal.

Jonas had told them how the meat that was taken out of pickle
would often be found sour, and how they would rub it up with soda to
ake away the smell, and sell it to be eaten on free-lunch counters;
lso of all the miracles of chemistry which they performed, giving to
ny sort of meat, fresh or salted, whole or chopped, any color and any
avor and any odor they chose. In the pickling of hams they had an
ngenious apparatus, by which they saved time and increased the capac-
ty of the plant—a machine consisting of a hollow needle attached to
 pump; by plunging this needle into the meat and working with his
oot, a man could fill a ham with pickle in a few seconds. And yet, in
pite of this, there would be hams found spoiled, some of them with
n odor so bad that a man could hardly bear to be in the room with
hem. To pump into these the packers had a second and much stronger
ickle which destroyed the odor—a process known to the workers as
giving them thirty per cent." Also, after the hams had been smoked,
here would be found some that had gone to the bad. Formerly these
ad been sold as "Number Three Grade," but later on some ingenious
erson had hit upon a new device, and now they would extract the
one, about which the bad part generally lay, and insert in the hole a
white-hot iron. After this invention there was no longer Number One,

Two, and Three Grade—there was only Number One Grade. The pac
ers were always originating such schemes—they had what they calle
"boneless hams," which were all the odds and ends of pork stuffed in
casings; and "California hams," which were the shoulders, with b
knuckle joints, and nearly all the meat cut out; and fancy "skinne
hams," which were made of the oldest hogs, whose skins were so heav
and coarse that no one would buy them—that is, until they had bee
cooked and chopped fine and labeled "head cheese!"

It was only when the whole ham was spoiled that it came into tl
department of Elzbieta. Cut up by the two-thousand-revolutions-a-mi
ute flyers, and mixed with half a ton of other meat, no odor th
ever was in a ham could make any difference. There was never tl
least attention paid to what was cut up for sausage; there would con
all the way back from Europe old sausage that had been rejected, ar
that was moldy and white—it would be dosed with borax and glycerin
and dumped into the hoppers, and made over again for home consum
tion. There would be meat that had tumbled out on the floor, in tl
dirt and sawdust, where the workers had tramped and spit uncount
billions of consumption germs. There would be meat stored in gre
piles in rooms; and the water from leaky roofs would drip over it, ar
thousands of rats would race about on it. It was too dark in these stora
places to see well, but a man could run his hand over these piles
meat and sweep off handfuls of the dried dung of rats. These rats we
nuisances, and the packers would put poisoned bread out for them; th
would die, and then rats, bread, and meat would go into the hoppe
together. This is no fairy story and no joke; the meat would be shovel
into carts, and the man who did the shoveling would not trouble
lift out a rat even when he saw one—there were things that went in
the sausage in comparison with which a poisoned rat was a tidbit. The
was no place for the men to wash their hands before they ate their di
ner, and so they made a practice of washing them in the water that w
to be ladled into the sausage. There were the butt-ends of smoked me
and the scraps of corned beef, and all the odds and ends of the waste
the plants, that would be dumped into old barrels in the cellar and le
there. Under the system of rigid economy which the packers enforce
there were some jobs that it only paid to do once in a long time, ar
among these was the cleaning out of the waste barrels. Every spring th
did it; and in the barrels would be dirt and rust and old nails and sta
water—and cartload after cartload of it would be taken up ar
dumped into the hoppers with fresh meat, and sent out to the publi
breakfast. Some of it they would make into "smoked" sausage—but

e smoking took time, and was therefore expensive, they would call
pon their chemistry department, and preserve it with borax and color
 with gelatine to make it brown. All of their sausage came out of
e same bowl, but when they came to wrap it they would stamp some
 it "special," and for this they would charge two cents more a pound.

Marie Van Vorst on
The Plight of the Working Woman
1903

Marie Van Vorst and her sister-in-law, Mrs. John Van Vorst, made separate expeditions into the life of the working girl, and together published accounts of their experiences. Explaining the effort that led to her masquerade as a working girl, Marie Van Vorst wrote: "I laid aside for a time everything pertaining to the class in which I was born and bred and became an American working-woman." Mrs. John Van Vorst and Marie Van Vorst, The Woman Who Toils: Being the Experiences of Two Gentlewomen as Factory Girls (*New York, 1903*), pp. 206-14.

The foreman was distinctly a personage. Small, kind, alive, he wore a straw hat and eye-glasses. He had decided in a moment that my short application for "something to do" was not to be gainsaid.

"Ever worked before?"

This time I had a branch of a trade at my fingers' ends.

"Yes, sir; presser."

I was proud of my trade.

I did not even know, as I do now, that "cleaning" is the filthiest jo the trade possesses. It is in bad repute and difficult to secure a woma to do the unpleasant work.

"You come with me," he said cheerfully; "I'll teach you."

The forelady at Parsons' did not know whether I worked well or no She never came to see. The foreman in Marches' taught me himself.

Two high desks, like old-time school desks, rose in the workshop centre. Behind one of these I stood, whilst the foreman in front of m instructed my ignorance. The room was filled with high crates rolle hither and thither on casters. These crates contained anywhere fror thirty-two to fifty pairs of boots. The cases are moved from operator t operator as each man selects the shoes to apply to them the especia branch of his trade. From the crate of boots rolled to my side I too four boots and placed them on the desk before me. With the heel o one pressed against my breast, I dipped my forefinger in a glass of ho soap and water, water which soon became black as ink. I passed my we soapy finger all around the boot's edges, from toe to heel. This loosenec in the space between the sole and vamp, the sticky dye substance o the leather and particles of so-called "dirt." Then with a bit of wood covered with Turkish toweling I scraped the shoe between the sole and vamp and with a third cloth polished and rubbed the boot clean. In an hour's time I did one-third as well as my companion. I cleaned a case in an hour, whilst she cleaned three.

When my employer had left me I observed the woman at my side: an untidy, degraded-looking creature, long past youth. Her hands beggared description; their covering resembled skin not at all, but a dark-blue substance, leatherlike, bruised, ingrained, indigo-hued. Her nails looked as though they had been beaten severely. One of her thumbs was bandaged.

"I lost one nail; rotted off."

"Horrible! How, pray?"

"That there water: it's poison from the shoe-dye."

Swiftly my hands were changing to a faint likeness of my companion's.

"Don't tell him," she said, "that I told you that. He'll be mad; he'll think I am discouraging you. But you'll lose your forefinger nail, all right!" Then she gave a little laugh as she turned her boot around to polish it.

"Once I tried to clean my hands up. Lord! it's no good! I scrub 'em with a scrubbin'-brush on Sundays."

"How long have you been at this job?"

"Ten months."

They called her "Bobby"; the men from their machines nodded to her now and then, bantering her across the noise of their wheels. She was ignorant of it, too stupid to know whether life took her in sport or in earnest! The men themselves worked in their flannel shirts. Not far from us was a wretchedly ill-looking individual, the very shadow of manhood. I observed that once he cast toward us a look of interest. Under my feet was a raised platform on which I stood, bending to my work. During the morning the consumptive man strolled over and whispered something to "Bobby." He made her dullness understand. When he had gone back to his job she said to me:

"Say, w'y don't yer push that platform away and stand down on the floor? You're too tall to need that. It makes yer bend."

"Did that man come over to tell you this?"

"Yes. He said it made you tired."

From my work, across the room, I silently blessed the pale old man, bowed, thin, pitiful, over the shoe he held, obscured from me by the cloud of sawdust-like flying leather that spun scattered from the sole he held to the flying wheel.

I don't believe the shoe-dye really to be poisonous. I suppose it is scarcely possible that it can be so; but the constant pressure against forefinger nail is enough to induce disease. My fingers were swollen sore. The effects of the work did not leave my hands for weeks.

"Bobby" was not talkative or communicative simply because she had nothing to say. Over and over again she repeated the one single question to me during the time I worked by her side: "Do you like your job?" and although I varied my replies as well as I could with the not too exhausting topic she offered, I could not induce her to converse. She took no interest in my work, absorbed in her own. Every now and then she would compute the sum she had made, finally deciding that the day was to be a red-bean day and she would make a dollar and fifty cents. During the time we worked together she had cleaned seventeen cases of shoes.

In this shop it was hotter than in Parsons'. We sweltered at our work. Once a case of shoes was cleaned, I wrote my initial "B" on the tag and rolled the crate across the floor to the man next me, who took it into his active charge.

The foreman came to me many times to inspect, approve and encourage. He was a model teacher and an indefatigable superintendent. Just how far personal, and just how far human, his kindness, who can say?

"You've been a presser long at the shoe-shops?"

"No."

"I like your pluck. When a girl has never had to work, and takes hold the way you do, I admire it. You will get along all right."

"Thank you; perhaps I won't, though."

"Now, don't get nervous. I am nervous myself," he said; "I know how that is."

On his next visit he asked me: "Where you goin' to when you get out of here to-night?"

I told him that I was all right—that I had a place to stay.

"If you're hard up, don't get discouraged; come to me."

I thanked him again and said that I could not take charity.

"Nonsense! I don't call it charity! If I was hard put, don't you s'pose I'd go to the next man if he offered me what I offer you? The world owes you a livin'."

When the foreman had left me I turned to look at "Bobby." She was in the act of lifting to her lips a glass of what was supposed to be water.

"You're not going to drink that!" I gasped, horrified. "Where did you get it?"

"Oh, I drawed it awhile ago," she said.

It had stood gathering microbes in the room, visible ones evidently, for a scum had formed on the glass that looked like stagnant oil. She blew the stuff back and drank long. Her accent was so bad and her English so limited I took her to be a foreigner beyond doubt. She proved to be an American. She had worked in factories all her life, since she was eight years old, and her brain was stunted.

At dinner time, when I left Marches', I had stood, without sitting down once, for five hours, and according to Bobby's computation I had made the large sum of twenty-five cents, having cleaned a little more than one hundred shoes. To all intents, at least for the moment, my hands were ruined. At Weyman's restaurant I went in with my fellow workwomen and men.

Weyman's restaurant smells very like the steerage in a vessel. The top floor having burned out a few weeks before, the ceiling remained blackened and filthy. The place was so close and foul-smelling that eating was an ordeal. If I had not been so famished, it would have been impossible for me to swallow a mouthful. I bought soup and beans, and ate, in spite of the inconveniences, ravenously, and paid for my dinner fifteen cents. Most of my neighbours took one course, stew or soup. I rose half-satisfied, dizzy from the fumes and the bad air. I am safe in saying that I never smelled anything like to Weyman's, and I hope never to again. Never again shall I hear food and drink discussed by the *gourmet*—discuss, indeed, with him over his repast—but there shall rise before me Weyman's restaurant, low-ceiled, foul, crowded to overflowing. I shall see the diners bend edged appetites to the unpalatable food. These Weyman patrons, mark well, are the rich ones, the swells of labour—able to squander fifteen to twenty cents on their stew and tea. There are dozens, you remember, still in the unaired fourth and fifth stories—at "lunching" over their sandwiches. Far more vivid, more poignant even must be to me the vision of "Bobby." I shall see her eat her filthy sandwich with her blackened hands, see her stoop to blow the scum of deadly matter from her typhoid-breeding glass.

In Lynn, unless she boards at home, a girl's living costs her at best $3.75 a week. If she be of the average* her month's earnings are $32. Reduce this by general expenses and living and her surplus is $16, to earn which she has toiled 224 hours. You will recall that there are, out

---

* Lynn's average wages are $8 per week.

of the 22,000 operatives in Massachusetts, 5,000 who make under $5 a week. I leave the reader to compute from this the luxuries and possible pleasures consistent with this income.

A word for the swells of the trade, for swells exist. One of my companions at 28 Viger Street made $14 a week. Her expenses were $4; she therefore had at her disposition about $40 a month. She had no family—*every cent of her surplus she spent on her clothes.*

"I like to look down and see myself dressed nice," she said; "it makes me feel good. I don't like myself in poor clothes."

She *was* well-dressed—her furs good, her hat charming. We walked to work side by side, she the lady of us. Of course she belongs to the Union. Her possible illness is provided for; her death will bring $100 to a distant cousin. She is only tired out, thin, undeveloped, pale, that's all. She is almost a capitalist, and extremely well dressed.

Poor attire, if I can judge by the reception I met with in Lynn, influences only those who by reason of birth, breeding and education should be above such things. In Viger Street I was more simply clad than my companions. My aspect called forth only sisterhood and kindness.

Fellowship from first to last, fellowship from their eyes to mine, a spark kindled never to be extinguished. The morning I left my tenement lodging Mika took my hand at the door.

"Good-by." Her eyes actually filled. "I'm awful sorry you're going. If the world don't treat you good come back to us."

I must qualify a little. One member of the working class there was on whom my cheap clothes had a chilling effect—the spoiled creature of the traveling rich, a Pullman car porter on the train from Boston to New York! Although I called him first and purposely gave him my order in time, he viewed me askance and served me the last of all. As I watched my companions in their furs and handsome attire eat, whilst I sat and waited, my woolen gloves folded in my lap, I wondered if any one of the favoured was as hungry, as famished as the presser from Parsons', the cleaner from Marches'.

John Spargo on
Child Labor
1906

"This great nation in its commercial madness devours its babes,"
John Spargo charged in his study of The Bitter Cry of the Children.
And in a work replete with horrifying detail, he documented his
case, and gave a strong impetus to the movement against child labor.
The basic accuracy of his findings was confirmed a few years later
in the nineteen volumes of the U. S. Bureau of Labor's Report on
Condition of Woman and Child Wage Earners in the United States.
Nationwide efforts to curb such abuses of children made slow
ground, however, largely because of decisions of the Supreme Court
invalidating national child labor laws and the inability of reformers
to secure the passage of a constitutional amendment on the subject.
John Spargo, The Bitter Cry of the Children *(New York, 1906),*
pp. 148-53, 163-67.

The textile industries rank first in the enslavement of children. In
the cotton trade, for example, 13.3 per cent of all persons employed
throughout the United States are under sixteen years of age. In the
Southern states, where the evil appears at its worst, so far as the textile
trades are concerned, the proportion of employees under sixteen years of
age in 1900 was 25.1 per cent, in Alabama the proportion was nearly
30 per cent. A careful estimate made in 1902 placed the number of
cotton-mill operatives under sixteen years of age in the Southern states
at 50,000. At the beginning of 1903 a very conservative estimate placed
the number of children under fourteen employed in the cotton mills of
the South at 30,000, no less than 20,000 of them being under twelve. If
this latter estimate of 20,000 children under twelve is to be relied upon,
it is evident that the total number under fourteen must have been
much larger than 30,000. According to Mr. McKelway, one of the most
competent authorities in the country, there are at the present time not
less than 60,000 children under fourteen employed in the cotton mills
of the Southern states. Miss Jane Addams tells of finding a child of five
years working by night in a South Carolina mill; Mr. Edward Gardner
Murphy has photographed little children of six and seven years who
were at work for twelve and thirteen hours a day in Alabama mills. In
Columbia, S. C., and Montgomery, Ala., I have seen hundreds of chil-

dren, who did not appear to be more than nine or ten years of age, at work in the mills, by night as well as by day.

The industrial revival in the South from the stagnation consequent upon the Civil War has been attended by the growth of a system of child slavery almost as bad as that which attended the industrial revolution in England a century ago. From 1880 to 1900 the value of the products of Southern manufactures increased from less than $458,000,000 to $1,463,000,000—an increase of 220 per cent. Many factors contributed to that immense industrial development of the South, but, according to a well-known expert, it is due "chiefly to her supplies of tractable and cheap labor." During the same period of twenty years in the cotton mills outside of the South, the proportion of workers under sixteen years of age decreased from 15.6 per cent to 7.7 per cent, but in the South it remained at approximately 25 per cent. It is true that the terrible pauper apprentice system which forms such a tragic chapter in the history of the English factory movement has not been introduced; yet the fate of the children of the poor families from the hill districts who have been drawn into the vortex of this industrial development is almost as bad as that of the English pauper children. These "poor whites," as they are expressively called, even by their negro neighbors, have for many years eked out a scanty living upon their farms, all the members of the family uniting in the struggle against niggardly nature. Drawn into the current of the new industrial order, they do not realize that, even though the children worked harder upon the farms than they do in the mills, there is an immense difference between the dust-laden air of a factory and the pure air of a farm; between the varied tasks of farm life with the endless opportunities for change and individual initiative, and the strained attention and monotonous tasks of mill life. The lot of the pauper children driven into the mills by the ignorance and avarice of British Bumbledom was little worse than that of these poor children, who work while their fathers loaf. During the long, weary nights many children have to be kept awake by having cold water dashed on their faces, and when morning comes they throw themselves upon their beds—often still warm from the bodies of their brothers and sisters—without taking off their clothing. "When I works nights, I'se too tired to undress when I gits home, an' so I goes to bed wif me clo's on me," lisped one little girl in Augusta, Ga.

There are more than 80,000 children employed in the textile industries of the United States, according to the very incomplete census returns, most of them being little girls. In these industries conditions are undoubtedly worse in the Southern states than elsewhere, though I have witnessed many pitiable cases of child slavery in Northern mills which equalled almost anything I have ever seen in the South. During the Philadelphia textile workers' strike in 1903, I saw at least a score of children ranging from eight to ten years of age who had been working in the mills prior to the strike. One little girl of nine I saw in the Kensington Labor Lyceum. She had been working for almost a year before the strike began, she said, and careful inquiry proved her story to be true. When "Mother" Mary Jones started with her little "army" of child toilers to march to Oyster Bay, in order that the President of the United States might see for himself some of the little ones who had actually been employed in the mills of Philadelphia, I happened to be engaged in assisting the strikers. For two days I accompanied the little "army" on its march, and thus had an excellent opportunity of studying the children. Amongst them were several from eight to eleven years of age, and I remember one little girl who was not quite eleven telling me with pride that she had "worked two years and never missed a day."

One evening, not long ago, I stood outside of a large flax mill in Paterson, N. J., while it disgorged its crowd of men, women, and children employees. All the afternoon, as I lingered in the tenement district near the mills, the comparative silence of the streets oppressed me. There were many babies and very small children, but the older children, whose boisterous play one expects in such streets, were wanting. "If thow'lt bide till th' mills shut for th' day, thow'lt see plenty on 'em —big kids as plenty as small taties," said one old woman to whom I spoke about it. She was right. At six o'clock the whistles shrieked, and the streets were suddenly filled with people, many of them mere children. Of all the crowd of tired, pallid, and languid-looking children I could only get speech with one, a little girl who claimed thirteen years, though she was smaller than many a child of ten. Indeed, as I think of her now, I doubt whether she would have come up to the standard of normal physical development either in weight or stature for a child of ten. One learns, however, not to judge the ages of working children by their physical appearance, for they are usually behind other children in height, weight, and girth of chest,—often as much as two or three years. If my little Paterson friend was thirteen, perhaps the nature of her employment will explain her puny, stunted body. She works in the "steaming room" of the flax mill. All day long, in a room filled with clouds of steam, she has to stand barefooted in pools of water twisting coils of wet hemp. When I saw her she was dripping wet, though she said that she had worn a rubber apron all day. In the coldest evenings of winter little Marie, and hundreds of other little girls, must go out from the superheated steaming rooms into the bitter cold in just that condition. No wonder that such children are stunted and underdeveloped!

In textile mill towns like Biddeford, Me., Manchester, N. H., Fall River and Lawrence, Mass., I have seen many such children, who, if they were twelve or fourteen according to their certificates and the companies' registers, were not more than ten or twelve in reality. I have watched them hurrying into and away from the mills, "those receptacles, in too many instances, for living human skeletons, almost disrobed of intellect," as Robert Owen's burning phrase describes them. I do not doubt that, upon the whole, conditions in the textile industries are better in the North than in the South, but they are nevertheless too bad to permit of self-righteous boasting and complacency. And in several other departments of industry conditions are no whit better in the North than in the South. The child-labor problem is not sectional, but national. . . .

According to the census of 1900, there were 25,000 boys under sixteen years of age employed in and around the mines and quarries of the United States. In the state of Pennsylvania alone,—the state which enslaves more children than any other,—there are thousands of little "breaker boys" employed, many of them not more than nine or ten years old. The law forbids the employment of children under fourteen, and the records of the mines generally show that the law is "obeyed." Yet in May, 1905, an investigation by the National Child Labor Committee showed that in one small borough of 7000 population, among the boys employed in breakers 35 were nine years old, 40 were ten, 45 were eleven, and 45 were twelve—over 150 boys illegally employed in one section of boy labor in one small town! . . .

Work in the coal breakers is exceedingly hard and dangerous. Crouched over the chutes, the boys sit hour after hour, picking out the pieces of slate and other refuse from the coal as it rushes past to the washers. From the cramped position they have to assume, most of them become more or less deformed and bent-backed like old men. When a boy has been working for some time and begins to get round-shouldered, his fellows say that "He's got his boy to carry round wherever he goes." The coal is hard, and accidents to the hands, such as cut, broken, or crushed fingers, are common among the boys. Sometimes there is a worse accident: a terrified shriek is heard, and a boy is mangled and torn in the machinery, or disappears in the chute to be picked out later smothered and dead. Clouds of dust fill the breakers and are inhaled by the boys, laying the foundations for asthma and miners' consumption. I once stood in a breaker for half an hour and tried to do the work a twelve-year-old boy was doing day after day, for ten hours at a stretch, for sixty cents a day. The gloom of the breaker appalled me. Outside the sun shone brightly, the air was pellucid, and the birds sang in chorus with the trees and the rivers. Within the breaker there was blackness, clouds of deadly dust enfolded everything, the harsh, grinding roar of the machinery and the ceaseless rushing of coal through the chutes filled the ears. I tried to pick out the pieces of slate from the hurrying stream of coal, often missing them; my hands were bruised and cut in a few minutes; I was covered from head to foot with coal dust, and for many hours afterwards I was expectorating some of the small particles of anthracite I had swallowed.

I could not do that work and live, but there were boys of ten and twelve years of age doing it for fifty and sixty cents a day. Some of them had never been inside of a school; few of them could read a child's primer. True, some of them attended the night schools, but after working ten hours in the breaker the educational results from attending school were practically *nil*. "We goes fer a good time, an' we keeps de guys wots dere hoppin' all de time," said little Owen Jones, whose work I had been trying to do. How strange that barbaric patois sounded to me as I remembered the rich, musical language I had so often heard other little Owen Joneses speak in faraway Wales. As I stood in that breaker I thought of the reply of the small boy to Robert Owen. Visiting an English coal-mine one day, Owen asked a twelve-year-old lad if he knew God. The boy stared vacantly at his questioner: "God?" he said, "God? No, I don't. He must work in some other mine." It was hard to realize amid the danger and din and blackness of that Pennsylvania breaker that such a thing as belief in a great All-good God existed.

From the breakers the boys graduate to the mine depths, where they become door tenders, switch-boys, or mule-drivers. Here, far below the surface, work is still more dangerous. At fourteen or fifteen the boys assume the same risks as the men, and are surrounded by the same perils. Nor is it in Pennsylvania only that these conditions exist. In the bituminous mines of West Virginia, boys of nine or ten are frequently employed. I met one little fellow ten years old in Mt. Carbon, W. Va., last year, who was employed as a "trap boy." Think of what it means to be a trap boy at ten years of age. It means to sit alone in a dark mine passage hour after hour, with no human soul near; to see no living creature except the mules as they pass with their loads, or a rat or two seeking to share one's meal; to stand in water or mud that covers the ankles, chilled to the marrow by the cold draughts that rush in when you open the trap-door for the mules to pass through; to work for fourteen hours—waiting—opening and shutting a door—then waiting again—for sixty cents; to reach the surface when all is wrapped in the mantle of night, and to fall to the earth exhausted and have to be carried away to the nearest "shack" to be revived before it is possible to walk to the farther shack called "home."

Boys twelve years of age may be *legally* employed in the mines of West Virginia, by day or by night, and for as many hours as the employers care to make them toil or their bodies will stand the strain. Where the disregard of child life is such that this may be done openly and with legal sanction, it is easy to believe what miners have again and again told me—that there are hundreds of little boys of nine and ten years of age employed in the coal-mines of this state.

Ray Stannard Baker on
The Condition of the Negro

February, 1905

*In the fall of 1904, Ray Stannard Baker investigated lynching in the
South and the North, as a prelude to a general study of the condition of the Negro in American life. A series of articles, published
in the* American Magazine *and* McClure's, *was later collected in an
illuminating book,* Following the Color Line *(1908). In his account,
Baker spared neither the North nor the South. The following
selection, which deals with the circumstances of a lynching in Springfield, Ohio, is representative of his effort to bring criticism to bear
not merely upon lynch mobs but also upon officers of the law who
failed to enforce it. Ray Stannard Baker, "What Is Lynching? A
Study of Mob Justice, South and North," McClure's, February, 1905.*

I cite these facts to show the underlying conditions in Springfield; a
soil richly prepared for an outbreak of mob law—with corrupt politics,
vile saloons, the law paralysed by non-enforcement against vice, a large
venal Negro vote, lax courts of justice.

GATHERING OF THE LYNCHING MOB

Well, on Monday afternoon the mob began to gather. At first it was
an absurd, ineffectual crowd, made up largely of lawless boys of sixteen
to twenty—a pronounced feature of every mob—with a wide fringe of
more respectable citizens, their hands in their pockets and no convictions in their souls, looking on curiously, helplessly. They gathered
hooting around the jail, cowardly, at first, as all mobs are, but growing
bolder as darkness came on and no move was made to check them. The
murder of Collis was not a horrible, soul-rending crime like that at
Statesboro, Georgia; these men in the mob were not personal friends of
the murdered man; it was a mob from the back rooms of the swarming
saloons of Springfield; and it included also the sort of idle boys "who
hang around cigar stores," as one observer told me. The newspaper
reports are fond of describing lynching mobs as "made up of the foremost citizens of the town." In no cases that I know of, either South or
North, . . . has a mob been made up of what may be called the best
citizens; but the best citizens have often stood afar off "decrying the
mob"—as a Springfield man told me piously—and letting it go on. A

mob is the method by which good citizens turn over the law and th
government to the criminal or irresponsible classes.

And no official in direct authority in Springfield that evening, ap
parently, had so much as an ounce of grit within him. The sheriff cam
out and made a weak speech in which he said he "didn't want to hur
anybody." They threw stones at him and broke his windows. The chie
of police sent eighteen men to the jail but did not go near himself. Al
of these policemen undoubtedly sympathised with the mob in its effort
to get at the slayer of their brother officer; at least, they did nothin
effective to prevent the lynching. An appeal was made to the Mayor t
order out the engine companies that water might be turned on th
mob. He said he didn't like to; *the hose might be cut!* The local militi
company was called to its barracks, but the officer in charge hesitated
vacillated, doubted his authority, and objected finally because he ha
no ammunition *except* Krag-Jorgenson cartridges, which, if fired into
mob, would kill too many people! The soldiers did not stir that nigh
from the safe and comfortable precincts of their armory.

A sort of dry rot, a moral paralysis, seems to strike the administrator
of law in a town like Springfield. What can be expected of officer
who are not accustomed to enforce the law, or of a people not accu
tomed to obey it—or who make reservations and exceptions when the
do enforce it or obey it?

THREATS TO LYNCH THE JUDGES

When the sheriff made his speech to the mob, urging them to let th
law take its course they jeered him. The law! When, in the past, ha
the law taken its proper course in Clark County? Someone shouted
referring to Dixon:

"He'll only get fined for shooting in the city limits."

"He'll get ten days in jail and suspended sentence."

Then there were voices:

"Let's go hang Mower and Miller"—the two judges.

This threat, indeed, was frequently repeated both on the night of th
lynching and on the day following.

So the mob came finally, and cracked the door of the jail with a rail
road rail. This jail is said to be the strongest in Ohio, and having seer
it, I can well believe that the report is true. But steel bars have neve
yet kept out a mob; it takes something a good deal stronger: huma
courage backed up by the consciousness of being right.

They murdered the Negro in cold blood in the jail doorway; the they dragged him to the principal business street and hung him to a telegraph-pole, afterward riddling his lifeless body with revolver shots.

LESSON OF A HANGING NEGRO

That was the end of that! Mob justice administered! And there the Negro hung until daylight the next morning—an unspeakably grisly, dangling horror, advertising the shame of the town. His head was shockingly crooked to one side, his ragged clothing, cut for souvenirs, exposed in places his bare body: he dripped blood. And, with the crowds of men both here and at the morgue where the body was publicly exhibited, came young boys in knickerbockers, and little girls and women by scores, horrified but curious. They came even with baby carriages! Men made jokes: "A dead nigger is a good nigger." And the purblind, dollars-and-cents man, most despicable of all, was congratulating the public:
"It'll save the county a lot of money!"
Significant lessons, these, for the young!
But the mob wasn't through with its work. Easy people imagine that, having hanged a Negro, the mob goes quietly about its business; but that is never the way of the mob. Once released, the spirit of anarchy spreads and spreads, not subsiding until it has accomplished its full measure of evil.

MOB BURNING OF NEGRO SALOONS

All the following day a rumbling, angry crowd filled the streets of Springfield, threatening to burn out the notorious Levee, threatening Judges Mower and Miller, threatening the "niggers." The local troops—to say nothing of the police force—which might easily have broken up the mob, remained sedulously in their armories, vacillating, doubtful of authority, knowing that there were threats to burn and destroy, and making not one move toward the protection of the public. One of the captains was even permitted to go to a neighboring city to a dance! At the very same time the panic-stricken officials were summoning troops from other towns. So night came on, the mob gathered around the notorious dives, someone touched a match, and the places of crime suddenly disgorged their foul inhabitants. Black and white, they came pouring out and vanished into the darkness where they belonged and whence they have not yet returned. Eight buildings went up in smoke, the fire department deliberating—intentionally, it is said—until the flames could not be controlled. The troops, almost driven out by the county prosecutor, McGrew, appeared after the mob had completed its work.

Good work, badly done, a living demonstration of the inevitability of law—if not orderly, decent law, then of mob-law.

For days following the troops filled Springfield, costing the state large sums of money, costing the county large sums of money. They chiefly guarded the public fountain; the mob had gone home—until next time.

EFFORTS TO PUNISH THE MOB

What happened after that? A perfunctory court-martial that did absolutely nothing. A grand jury of really good citizens that sat for weeks off and on; and like the mountain that was in travail and brought forth a mouse, they indicted two boys and two men out of all that mob, not for murder but for "breaking into jail." And, curiously enough, it developed—how do such things develop?—that every man on the grand jury was a Republican, chosen by Republican county officers, and in their report they severely censored police force (Democratic), and the mayor (Democratic), and had not one word of disapproval for the sheriff (Republican). Curiously enough, also, the public did not become enthusiastic over the report of that grand jury. . . .

But the worst feature of all in this Springfield lynching was the apathy of the public. No one really seemed to care. A "nigger" had been hanged what of it? But the law itself had been lynched. What of that? I had just come from the South, where I had found the people of several lynching towns in a state of deep excitement—moral excitement if you like thinking about this problem, quarrelling about it, expelling men from the church, impeaching sheriffs, dishonourably discharging whole militia companies. Here in Springfield, I found cold apathy, except for a few fine citizens, one of whom City Solicitor Stewart L. Tatum, promptly offered his services to the sheriff and assisted in a vain effort to remove the Negro in a closed carriage and afterward at the risk of personal assault earnestly attempted to defeat the purposes of the mob. Another of these citizens, the Rev. Father Cogan, pleaded with the mob on the second night of the rioting at risk to himself; another withdrew from the militia company because it had not done its duty. And afterward the city officials were stirred by the faintest of faint spasms of righteousness some of the Negro saloons were closed up, but within a month, the most notorious of all the dive-keepers, Hurley, the Negro political boss, was permitted to open an establishment—through the medium of a brother in-law!

If there ever was an example of good citizenship lying flat on its back with political corruption squatting on its neck, Springfield furnished an example of that condition.

PART TWO

Social and Moral Issues

An East-Side Resident Testifies
On Tenement Conditions

November 26, 1900

*The thorough investigation conducted by the New York Tene-
ment House Commission into tenement conditions in 1900 led to
the passage the following year of the New York Tenement House
Law, which set higher standards for buildings to be constructed. In
the next fifteen years eleven states and more than forty cities passed
tenement house codes, usually modeled after the New York statute, or
revised old ones. But the enactment of such laws was only the prelude to a long battle for enforcement. Here Mr. Henry Moscowitz,
a knowledgeable tenement-dweller, is sympathetically questioned
by Lawrence Veiller, the secretary of the Commission. Robert W.
De Forest and Lawrence Veiller, eds.,* The Tenement House Problem
(New York, 1903), Vol. I, pp. 412-417.

Mr. Henry Moscowitz then took the witness chair and was interrogated
by the secretary:
The Secretary.—Where do you reside?
Mr. Moscowitz.—95 Forsyth Street.
The Secretary.—Is that a tenement house?
Mr. Moscowitz.—Yes, sir.
The Secretary.—How long have you lived in tenement houses?
Mr. Moscowitz.—Seventeen years.
The Secretary.—Practically most of your life?
Mr. Moscowitz.—Yes, sir.
The Secretary.—In that time do you remember about how many tene-
ment houses you have lived in?
Mr. Moscowitz.—Fourteen.
The Secretary.—Fourteen different buildings?
Mr. Moscowitz.—Yes, sir.
The Secretary.—So that you feel you are competent to speak on the
condition of tenement houses from your own experience?

Mr. Moscowitz.—Yes, sir.

The Secretary.—Have you resided generally in one part of the city?

Mr. Moscowitz.—Yes; in the lower East Side.

The Secretary.—What have you got to say about the air shaft; do you think it is a good thing?

Mr. Moscowitz.—I think it is decidedly a bad thing. I must confirm the statements by other witnesses that the air shaft is a breeder of disease, and especially that there can be no fresh air in any building with an air shaft, from my experience, because of the refuse thrown down in the air shaft, the stench is so vile and the air is so foul that the occupants do not employ the windows as a means of getting air.

The Secretary.—Do these shafts furnish light to the rooms, in your experience?

Mr. Moscowitz.—They do not. They do not furnish light because the windows are very often dirty. That is one thing; they are not cleaned by the tenants very often and I will explain it that it is a hopeless task; the windows cannot be made clean during the day.

The Secretary.—Why is that?

Mr. Moscowitz.—Well, there is dirt and dust comes down the walls and strikes the windows.

The Secretary.—Do you mean from the apartments above?

Mr. Moscowitz.—Apartments above.

The Secretary.—People shake things out of the windows?

Mr. Moscowitz.—Yes, and throw things.

The Secretary.—That is not the fault of the air shaft, but of the tenants?

Mr. Moscowitz.—Yes, sir.

The Secretary.—Are there any other objections to the air shaft?

Mr. Moscowitz.—It destroys privacy.

The Secretary.—How does it do that?

Mr. Moscowitz.—I know where I lived in a house where there was a family opposite, the windows which are usually diagonal, I heard everything, especially loud noises, and when the windows are not covered one sees into the house.

The Secretary.—You have observed that in numbers of cases?

Mr. Moscowitz.—I have observed that in every case.

The Secretary.—Do you think that the tenement houses should be restricted in height?

Mr. Moscowitz.—Decidedly. I think that no tenement house ought to be built over five stories high. It is injurious to the health of the women.

The Secretary.—In what way?

Mr. Moscowitz.—The women complain, and I know this to be a fact, there is a Jewish word "stiegen," the stairs. Families who live on the third floor complain that they have to go up and down, and I know that many a woman has complained of the side ache to me because of the "stiegen."

The Secretary.—Is it true that because of the stairs many of the women in the tenement houses seldom go down into the street and outdoors?

Mr. Moscowitz.—Decidedly true. I know this for a fact; that they do not visit their neighbors often. Complaints, serious complaints are made, "Why don't you come to visit me?" and they say "We live so high up we seldom come."

The Secretary.—Do you know of many families where the mother does not go out oftener than twice a week?

Mr. Moscowitz.—I do.

The Secretary.—Would you say that was a very general practice?

Mr. Moscowitz.—Very general, yes.

The Secretary.—You think that has a bad effect on the health of the people?

Mr. Moscowitz.—Very bad effect.

The Secretary.—Are there any other reasons why you object to tall buildings?

Mr. Moscowitz.—I think the children are kept in the street a good deal; the parents, especially the mother, very often loses sight of the children, and she has to open the windows and shout down for the little one at play when she wants it in the room, and the parents cannot trace the children; cannot keep track of them.

The Secretary.—Are the hallways in most tenement houses you have observed light or dark?

Mr. Moscowitz.—Dark.

The Secretary.—How dark?

Mr. Moscowitz.—Well, they are dark in most houses that I have lived in. One tumbles over human obstacles and other obstacles, especially little children.

The Secretary.—Are the rooms dark or light in most of the tenement houses you have lived in?

Mr. Moscowitz.—The bedrooms are dark. The kitchen and the front room called the parlor is light.

The Secretary.—Have you any recommendation to make with reference to baths on the East Side in tenement houses?

Mr. Moscowitz.—Yes, sir; I think that baths are very essential. Because there are no baths in the tenement houses many of the tenants do not bathe as often as they otherwise would. I can say from experience that many tenants do not bathe more than six times a year, and often less, and not because they would not take advantage of the opportunity, but there are no opportunities.

The Secretary.—Cannot they take a bath in the rooms?

Mr. Moscowitz.—No, they cannot. There are no baths there.

The Secretary.—Cannot they take a tub and bathe in that way?

Mr. Moscowitz.—Well, they may take a tub, but they do not do that very often.

The Secretary.—Why, is it difficult?

Mr. Moscowitz.—I believe it is difficult. The tubs are narrow in the tenements.

The Secretary.—You mean the wash-tubs?

Mr. Moscowitz.—The wash-tubs, yes.

The Secretary.—Have you ever seen a bath-tub in a tenement house?

Mr. Moscowitz.—Never.

The Secretary.—Never in seventeen years?

Mr. Moscowitz.—Never in seventeen years.

The Secretary.—It has been stated that bath-tubs, when put in tenement houses, have been used for the storage of coal. Have you ever heard of such a thing?

Mr. Moscowitz.—It is the same story I have heard time and time again.

The Secretary.—From your knowledge of the people do you think it is true?

Mr. Moscowitz.—It is decidedly not true.

The Secretary.—Is it not the fact that the people buy their coal mostly by the pail, so that they could not store it in bath-tubs?

Mr. Moscowitz.—That is true.

The Secretary.—Have you known of cases where the water supply in tenements has been deficient?

Mr. Moscowitz.—Yes, sir; in the summer-time very often the water supply is deficient, and people are deprived of water for half a day. I have known that to be the case in two instances of my own knowledge, and the particular water supply is deficient in tenements which have closets in the hallways. This is a fact which is general. From my own observations in the tenements where the closets are situated in the hall, the stench is very noticeable, and the reason, I believe, is because there is not a sufficient flush in the closet. I do not know whether it is compulsory for the landlord to supply a certain thickness of pipe, but I surely think it ought to be because I have noticed that the water supply is not sufficient in the closets situated in the hallways.

The Secretary.—Have you noticed the practice of people sleeping on the roofs and in the street in the summertime?

Mr. Moscowitz.—Yes, sir, I have, because I myself have done so.

The Secretary.—Why?

Mr. Moscowitz.—Because it was too hot to sleep in the room in the summer-time.

The Secretary.—Is this practice general?

Mr. Moscowitz.—It is general.

The Secretary.—What proportion would you say of the people in the summer-time sleep on the roofs and in the street?

Mr. Moscowitz.—I think about one-third of the people sleep on the roofs in my observation.

The Secretary.—And you attribute that entirely to the heat of the rooms?

Mr. Moscowitz.—Decidedly so, and to the air in the summertime.

The Secretary.—How often in seventeen years have you seen a sanitary inspector?

Mr. Moscowitz.—Never.

The Secretary.—How often have you seen a light burning in a dark hallway in the daytime?

Mr. Moscowitz.—I have a dim recollection of having seen one about twelve years ago in a tenement on Essex Street.

The Secretary.—Do you think the tenement house system is a good thing for the community?

Mr. Moscowitz.—A very bad thing for the community.

The Secretary.—Why?

Mr. Moscowitz.—Because, first, it destroys the privacy of the home. Then I believe the most serious thing is that it disintegrates the home.

The Secretary.—In what way?

Mr. Moscowitz.—The home is very unattractive for the children and they are glad to get out to meet their friends. They want to supply a social need, and they go out and meet other friends and the home has no tie upon them. The father—there is not the authority of the parent that existed in the old country, and I believe because the child is not at home as often as he should be. The tenement house is a decidedly disintegrating influence in the family, and that is seen especially on the East Side today.

The Secretary.—I have always understood that among the Jewish people the patriarchal form of government was very strong and the authority of the father very strong.

Mr. Moscowitz.—Yes.

The Secretary.—Do you mean to say that this is being weakened by the tenement houses?

Mr. Moscowitz.—The tenement house is not the only thing, but a very strong influence. I believe the entire economic conditions in this country are another influence, and I will state decidedly that I think the tenement house life is a strong influence in that direction.

The Secretary.—Would you have us infer from your statement that the young men and young women have to meet each other on the street because the home is unattractive?

Mr. Moscowitz.—Well, they meet each other on the streets, and in club-rooms, and in settlements, but very few I think meet each other there. In dancing academies, in social clubs, in balls and receptions.

The Secretary.—And you think this is a bad thing?

Mr. Moscowitz.—Decidedly a bad thing, because of another point, the tenement house life destroys a certain delicacy of feeling, which is noticeable in one brought up in a good home. That is a decided characteristic of the young men and women living in the tenement houses, that they are too socially dependent.

Robert Hunter on Poverty

1904

A social worker and a settlement resident of Socialist sympathies, Robert Hunter was one of the first American writers to try to combine the methods of systematic inquiry and of direct observation in the study of poverty. Although his assertion that as many as 10,000,000 persons in the United States lived in poverty even in prosperous times aroused great controversy, his plea for a recognition of the fact of poverty was immensely effective, and his study was widely read. Robert Hunter, Poverty *(New York, 1904), pp. 1-5, 337-40.*

William Dean Howells said to me recently, after I had told him of a visit to Tolstoy: "It is wonderful what Tolstoy has done. He could do no more. For a nobleman, with the most aristocratic ancestry, to refuse to be supported in idleness, to insist upon working with his own hands, and to share as much as possible the hardship and toil of a peasant class, which, but recently, was a slave class, is the greatest thing he could do. But it is impossible for him to share their poverty, for poverty is not the lack of things; it is the fear and the dread of want. That fear Tolstoy could not know." These remarks of Mr. Howells brought to mind the wonderful words of Thomas Carlyle: "It is not to die, or even to die of hunger, that makes a man wretched; many men have died; all men must die. . . . But it is to live miserable we know not why; to work sore and yet gain nothing; to be heart-worn, weary, yet isolated, unrelated, girt in with a cold, universal Laissez-faire." To live miserable we know not why, to have the dread of hunger, to work sore and yet gain nothing,—this is the essence of poverty.

There are many people in the world who believe that the provisions of charity are in the present day so generous and varied that no one need suffer; but, even if this were true, it would not materially lessen the sorrow of the poor. To thousands and thousands of working-men the dread of public pauperism is the agony of their lives. The mass of working-men on the brink of poverty hate charity. Not only their words convey a knowledge of this fact, but their actions, when in distress, make it absolutely undeniable. When the poor face the necessity of becoming paupers, when they must apply for charity if they are to live at all, many

desert their families and enter the ranks of vagrancy; others drink themselves insensible; some go insane; and still others commit suicide. Recently a man who had been unable to find work and in despair committed
suicide, left a note to his wife, saying: "I have gone forever; there is one
less in the world to feed. Good-by. God help you to care for Tony; don't
put her away." This is the fear and dread of pauperism; "don't put Tony
away" is the last thought of the man whose misery caused him to take
his own life.

These are the terrible alternatives which the working people in poverty
accept in preference to pauperism, and yet it is a curious fact, which
psychology alone explains, that the very men who will suffer almost anything rather than become paupers are often the very ones who never
care to be anything else when once they have become dependent upon
alms. When a family once become dependent, the mental agony which
they formerly had disappears. Paupers are not, as a rule, unhappy. They
are not ashamed; they are not keen to become independent; they are not
bitter or discontented. They have passed over the line which separates
poverty from pauperism.

This distinction between the poor and paupers may be seen everywhere. There are in all large cities in America and abroad, streets and
courts and alleys where a class of people live who have lost all self-respect
and ambition, who rarely, if ever, work, who are aimless and drifting
who like drink, who have no thought for their children, and who live
more or less contentedly on rubbish and alms. Such districts are certain
portions of Whitechapel and Spitalsfield, etc., in London, Kitrof Rynock
in Moscow, parts of Armour Avenue in Chicago, Rat Hollow in Cin
cinnati, and parts of Cherry Hill and the Minettas in New York City
and so on in all cities everywhere. The lowest level of humanity is reached
in these districts. In our American cities Negroes, Whites, Chinese, Mex
icans, Half-breeds, Americans, Irish, and others are indiscriminately
housed together in the same tenements and even in the same rooms
The blind, the crippled, the consumptive, the aged,—the ragged end
of life; the babies, the children, the half-starved, underclad beginnings ir
life, all huddled together, waiting, drifting. This is pauperism. There i
no mental agony here; they do not work sore; there is no dread; they
live miserably, but they do not care.

In the same cities and, indeed, everywhere, there are great districts o
people who are up before dawn, who wash, dress, and eat breakfast, kis
wives and children, and hurry away to work or to seek work. The worl
rests upon their shoulders; it moves by their muscle; everything would
stop if, for any reason, they should decide not to go into the fields and

ctories and mines. But the world is so organized that they gain enough
o live upon only when they work; should they cease, they are in destitu-
on and hunger. The more fortunate of the laborers are but a few weeks
om actual distress when the machines are stopped. Upon the unskilled
masses want is constantly pressing. As soon as employment ceases, suffer-
ig stares them in the face. They are the actual producers of wealth, who
ave no home nor any bit of soil which they may call their own. They
re the millions who possess no tools and can work only by permission
f another. In the main, they live miserably, they know not why. They
ork sore, yet gain nothing. They know the meaning of hunger and the
read of want. They love their wives and children. They try to retain
heir self-respect. They have some ambition. They give to neighbors in
eed, yet they are themselves the actual children of poverty. . . .

There are probably in fairly prosperous years no less than 10,000,000
ersons in poverty; that is to say, underfed, underclothed, and poorly
oused. Of these about 4,000,000 persons are public paupers. Over 2,000,-
00 working-men are unemployed from four to six months in the year.
bout 500,000 male immigrants arrive yearly and seek work in the very
istricts where unemployment is greatest. Nearly half of the families in
e country are propertyless. Over 1,700,000 little children are forced to
ecome wage-earners when they should still be in school. About 5,000,000
omen find it necessary to work and about 2,000,000 are employed in
ctories, mills, etc. Probably no less than 1,000,000 workers are injured
r killed each year while doing their work, and about 10,000,000 of the per-
ns now living will, if the present ratio is kept up, die of the preventable
isease, tuberculosis. We know that many workmen are overworked and
nderpaid. We know in a general way that unnecessary disease is far too
revalent. We know some of the insanitary evils of tenements and fac-
ries; we know of the neglect of the street child, the aged, the infirm,
e crippled. Furthermore, we are beginning to realize the monstrous in-
istice of compelling those who are unemployed, who are injured in in-
ustry, who have acquired diseases due to their occupation, or who have
een made widows or orphans by industrial accidents, to become paupers
order that they may be housed, fed, and clothed. Something is known
oncerning these problems of poverty, and some of them at least are possi-
e of remedy.

To deal with these specific problems, I have elsewhere mentioned some
forms which seem to me preventive in their nature. They contemplate
ainly such legislative action as may enforce upon the entire country
rtain minimum standards of working and of living conditions. They

would make all tenements and factories sanitary; they would regulat
the hours of work, especially for women and children; they would regu
late and thoroughly supervise dangerous trades; they would institute a
necessary measures to stamp out unnecessary disease and to prevent u
necessary death; they would prohibit entirely child labor; they wou
institute all necessary educational and recreational institutions to repla
the social and educational losses of the home and the domestic worksho
they would perfect, as far as possible, legislation and institutions to mak
industry pay the necessary and legitimate cost of producing and mai
taining efficient laborers; they would institute, on the lines of foreign e
perience, measures to compensate labor for enforced seasons of idlenes
due to sickness, old age, lack of work, or other causes beyond the contr
of the workman; they would prevent parasitism on the part of either th
consumer or the producer and charge up the full costs of labor in pr
duction to the beneficiary, instead of compelling the worker at certai
times to enforce his demand for maintenance through the tax rate an
by becoming a pauper; they would restrict the power of employer an
of ship-owner to stimulate for purely selfish ends an excessive immigr
tion, and in this way to beat down wages and to increase unemploymen

Reforms such as these are not ones which will destroy incentive, b
rather they will increase incentive by more nearly equalizing opportunit
They will make propertied interests less predatory, and sensuality, by co
trast with misery, less attractive to the poor. Or, in the terms of o
simile, the greyhound—which Dante promised would one day come-
will come to drive away the lion, the leopard, and the she-wolf. Th
does not mean that there is to be no struggle,—the mountain must st
remain,—but rather that the life of the poorest toiler shall not be
hopeless thing from which many must turn in despair. In other wor
the process of Justice is to lift stony barriers, against which the nobl
beat their brains out, and from which the ignoble (but who shall say n
more sensible?) turn away in despair. Let it be this, rather than a barr
relief system, administered by those who must stand by, watching t
struggle, lifting no hand to aid the toilers, but ever succoring those w
flee and those who are bruised and beaten.

Justice Holmes Dissents
in *Lochner* v. *New York*
1905

In the case of Lochner v. *New York, the Supreme Court found unconstitutional a New York law establishing a sixty-hour work week for bakers. Speaking for the Court in this five-to-four decision, Mr. Justice Peckham stigmatized the law as another instance of "mere meddlesome interferences with the rights of the individual," and found it contrary to those rights as protected by the Fourteenth Amendment. Although Justice Oliver Wendell Holmes, Jr. was by no means a typical Progressive in his thinking, his vigorously phrased dissent in this case made him the intellectual leader of liberal jurisprudence in the United States. This dissent, Roscoe Pound wrote four years later, was "the best exposition we have" of "the sociological movement in jurisprudence, the movement for pragmatism as a philosophy of law, the movement for the adjustment of principles and doctrines to the human conditions they are to govern rather than to assumed first principles, the movement for putting the human factor in the central place and relegating logic to its true position as an instrument." See also Docs. 11 and 12.* Lochner v. New York, *198 U. S. 45, 74.*

Holmes, J., dissenting. . . . The case is decided upon an economic theory which a large part of the country does not entertain. If it were a question whether I agreed with that theory, I should desire to study it further and long before making up my mind. But I do not conceive that to be my duty, because I strongly believe that my agreement or disagreement has nothing to do with the right of a majority to embody their opinions in law. It is settled by various decisions of this court that state constitutions and state laws may regulate life in many ways which we as legislators might think as injudicious, or if you like as tyrannical, as this, and which, equally with this, interfere with the liberty to contract. Sunday laws and usury laws are ancient examples. A more modern one is the prohibition of lotteries. The liberty of the citizen to do as he likes so long as he does not interfere with the liberty of others to do the same, which has been a shibboleth for some well-known writers, is interfered with by school laws, by the post-office, by every state or municipal institution which takes his money for purposes thought desirable, whether he likes it or not. The Fourteenth Amendment does not enact Mr. Herbert Spencer's Social Statics. . . . United States and state statutes and decisions cutting down the liberty to contract by way of combination are familiar to this court. . . . Some of these laws embody convictions or prejudices which judges are likely to share. Some may not. But a constitution is not intended to embody a particular economic theory, whether of paternalism and the organic relation of the citizen to the state or of *laissez faire*. It is made for people of fundamentally differing views, and the accident of our finding certain opinions natural and familiar, or novel and even shocking, ought not to conclude our judgment upon the question whether statutes embodying them conflict with the Constitution of the United States.

General propositions do not decide concrete cases. The decision will depend on a judgment or intuition more subtle than any articulate major premise. But I think that the proposition just stated, if it is accepted, will carry us far toward the end. Every opinion tends to become a law. I think that the word liberty in the Fourteenth Amendment is perverted when it is held to prevent the natural outcome of a dominant opinion, unless it can be said that a rational and fair man necessarily would admit that the statute proposed would infringe fundamental principles as they have been understood by the traditions of our people and our law. It does not need research to show that no such sweeping condemnation can be passed upon the statute before us. A reasonable man might think it a proper measure on the score of health. Men whom I certainly could not pronounce unreasonable would uphold it as a first instalment of a general regulation of the hours of work. Whether in the latter aspect it would be open to the charge of inequality I think it unnecessary to discuss.

Louis D. Brandeis Presents
An Unconventional Brief
1907

In the case of Muller *v.* Oregon *Louis D.* *Brandeis represented the state of Oregon, defending the constitutionality of a law establishing a ten-hour working day for women. In his brief, Brandeis gave relatively little attention to matters of law and concentrated heavily on matters of fact, piling up evidence from many kinds of sources to show that long hours of work are indeed dangerous to the health and safety of women. In the decision of the Court sustaining the law (Doc. 12) Justice Brewer took judicial cognizance of this aspect of his brief. Louis D. Brandeis,* Women in Industry *(New York, 1907), pp. 1, 10-11, 16-17, 18-21.*

This case . . . presents the single question whether the Statute of Oregon, . . . which provides that "no female [shall] be employed in any mechanical establishment or factory or laundry" "more than ten hours during any one day," is unconstitutional and void as violating the Fourteenth Amendment of the Federal Constitution.

The decision in this case will, in effect, determine the constitutionality of nearly all the statutes in force in the United States, limiting the hours of labor of adult women. . . .

The facts of common knowledge of which the Court may take judicial notice . . . establish, we submit, conclusively, that there is reasonable ground for holding that to permit women in Oregon to work in a "mechanical establishment, or factory, or laundry" more than ten hours in one day is dangerous to the public health, safety, morals, or welfare. . . .

The leading countries in Europe in which women are largely employed in factory or similar work have found it necessary to take action for the protection of their health and safety and the public welfare, and have enacted laws limiting the hours of labor of women. . . .

Twenty States of the Union . . . have enacted laws limiting the hours of labor for adult women. . . .

In the United States, as in foreign countries, there has been a general movement to strengthen and to extend the operation of these laws. In no State has any such law been held unconstitutional, except in Illinois. . . .

I. THE DANGERS OF LONG HOURS

A. *Causes*

(1) PHYSICAL DIFFERENCES BETWEEN MEN AND WOMAN

The dangers of long hours for women arise from their special physica organization taken in connection with the strain incident to factory and similar work.

Long hours of labor are dangerous for women primarily because o their special physical organization. In structure and function women are differentiated from men. Besides these anatomical and physiological dif ferences, physicians are agreed that women are fundamentally weaker than men in all that makes for endurance: in muscular strength, in nervous energy, in the powers of persistent attention and application Overwork, therefore, which strains endurance to the utmost, is more disastrous to the health of women than of men, and entails upon them more lasting injury.

REPORT OF SELECT COMMITTEE ON SHOPS EARLY CLOSING BILL,
BRITISH HOUSE OF COMMONS, 1895

Dr. Percy Kidd, physician in Brompton and London Hospitals:
The most common effect I have noticed of the long hours is genera deterioration of health; very general symptoms which we medically at tribute to over-action, and debility of the nervous system; that include a great deal more than what is called nervous disease, such as indigestion constipation, a general slackness, and a great many other indefinite symptoms.
Are those symptoms more marked in women than in men?
I think they are much more marked in women. I should say one see a great many more women of this class than men; but I have seen pre cisely the same symptoms in men, I should not say in the same propor tion, because one has not been able to make anything like a statistica inquiry. There are other symptoms, but I mention those as being the most common. Another symptom especially among women is anæmia

loodlessness or pallor, that I have no doubt is connected with long hours ndoors. (Page 215.)

REPORT OF COMMITTEE ON EARLY CLOSING OF SHOPS BILL, BRITISH HOUSE OF LORDS, 1901

Sir W. MacComac, President of the Royal College of Surgeons:
Would you draw a distinction between the evil resulting to women nd the evil resulting to men?
You see men have undoubtedly a greater degree of physical capacity han women have. Men are capable of greater effort in various ways than romen. If a like amount of physical toil and effort be imposed upon romen, they suffer to a larger degree. (Page 219.)

REPORT OF THE MAINE BUREAU OF INDUSTRIAL AND LABOR STATISTICS, 1888

Let me quote from Dr. Ely Van der Warker (1875):
Woman is badly constructed for the purposes of standing eight or ten ours upon her feet. I do not intend to bring into evidence the peculiar osition and nature of the organs contained in the pelvis, but to call at- ention to the peculiar construction of the knee and the shallowness of he pelvis, and the delicate nature of the foot as part of a sustaining olumn. The knee joint of woman is a sexual characteristic. Viewed in ront and extended, the joint in but a slight degree interrupts the gradual aper of the thigh into the leg. Viewed in a semi-flexed position, the joint orms a smooth ovate spheroid. The reason of this lies in the smallness f the patella in front, and the narrowness of the articular surfaces of the ibia and femur, and which in man form the lateral prominences, and hus is much more perfect as a sustaining column than that of a woman. The muscles which keep the body fixed upon the thighs in the erect osition labor under the disadvantage of shortness of purchase, owing to he short distance, compared to that of man, between the crest of the lium and the great trochanter of the femur, thus giving to man a much arger purchase in the leverage existing between the trunk and the ex- remities. Comparatively the foot is less able to sustain weight than that f man, owing to its shortness and the more delicate formation of the arsus and metatarsus. (Page 142.)

REPORT OF THE MASSACHUSETTS BUREAU OF LABOR STATISTICS,
1875

A "lady operator," many years in the business, informed us: "I hav
had hundreds of lady compositors in my employ, and they all exhibitec
in a marked manner, both in the way they performed their work and i
its results, the difference in physical ability between themselves and mer
They cannot endure the prolonged close attention and confinement whic
is a great part of type-setting. I have few girls with me more than two c
three years at a time; they must have vacations, and they break down i
health rapidly. I know no reason why a girl could not set as much type a
a man, if she were as strong to endure the demand on mind and body.
(Page 96.)

REPORT OF THE NEBRASKA BUREAU OF LABOR AND INDUSTRIAL
STATISTICS, 1901-1902

They (women) are unable, by reason of their physical limitations, t
endure the same hours of exhaustive labor as may be endured by adul
males. Certain kinds of work which may be performed by men withou
injury to their health would wreck the constitution and destroy th
health of women, and render them incapable of bearing their share c
the burdens of the family and the home. The State must be accorded th
right to guard and protect women as a class against such a conditior
and the law in question to that extent conserves the public health an
welfare. (Page 52.)

HYGIENE OF OCCUPATIONS. BY DR. THEODORE WEYL. JENA,
1894

The investigations of Schuler and Burkhardt embracing 18,000 men
bers of Swiss insurance against sickness (about 25 per cent of the Swis
factory workers and fifteen industries), show that factory work, even i
a short period, produces very unfavorable effects upon the developmen
of the body of young men. It is even more conspicuous in the case o
women. Thus of 1000 men in the manufacture of embroidery, 302 wer
sick to 332 women. In bleaching and dyeing, 279 men, 316 women; als
in cotton spinning and weaving, the morbidity of women was mucl
greater than of men.
Similarly the number of working days lost through illness was mor

nong women than among men, being 6.47 among women to 6.25 among
en.

With increasing years, both frequency and duration of illness increase.
'age 7.) . . .

David J. Brewer in
Muller v. *Oregon*

1908

*In this case, the Court was far more sympathetic to a law regulating
hours of work than it had been in the Lochner case (Doc. 10), for it
responded to Brandeis' impressive brief (Doc. 11) by sustaining the
Oregon law. Since this decision related specifically to the number of
hours worked by* women, *it could not be taken as overruling* Lochner
v. New York, *though it betokened a change of heart. Nine years
afterward, in* Bunting v. Oregon *(1917) the Court went all the way
and upheld a ten-hour law affecting both men and women.* Muller
v. Oregon, *208 U. S. 412.*

Brewer, J. . . . The single question is the constitutionality of the stat
ute under which the defendant was convicted, so far as affects the wor
of a female in a laundry. . . .

It is the law of Oregon that women, whether married or single, hav
equal contractual and personal rights with men. . . .

It thus appears that, putting to one side the elective franchise, in th
matter of personal and contractual rights they stand on the same plan
as the other sex. Their rights in these respects can no more be infringe
than the equal rights of their brothers. We held in *Lochner* v. *New York*
198 U. S. 45, that a law providing that no laborer shall be required o
permitted to work in a bakery more than sixty hours in a week or te
hours in a day was not as to men a legitimate exercise of the police powe
of the State, but an unreasonable, unnecessary, and arbitrary interferenc
with the right and liberty of the individual to contract in relation to hi
labor, and as such was in conflict with, and void under, the federal Con
stitution. That decision is invoked by plaintiff in error as decisive of th
question before us. But this assumes that the difference between the sexe
does not justify a different rule respecting a restriction of the hours o
labor.

It may not be amiss, in the present case, before examining the consti
tutional question, to notice the course of legislation as well as expression
of opinion from other than judicial sources. In the brief filed by Mr
Louis D. Brandeis for the defendant in error is a very copious collectio
of all these matters. . . .

The legislation and opinions referred to [in the Brandeis brief] . .

may not be, technically speaking, authorities, and in them is little or no discussion of the constitutional question presented to us for determination, yet they are significant of a wide-spread belief that woman's physical structure, and the functions she performs in consequence thereof, justify special legislation restricting or qualifying the conditions under which she should be permitted to toil. Constitutional questions, it is true, are not settled by even a consensus of present public opinion, for it is the peculiar value of a written constitution that it places in unchanging form limitations upon legislative action, and thus gives a permanence and stability to popular government which otherwise would be lacking. At the same time, when a question of fact is debated and debatable, and the extent to which a special constitutional limitation goes is affected by the truth in respect to that fact, a widespread and long-continued belief concerning it is worthy of consideration. We take judicial cognizance of all matters of general knowledge. . . .

That woman's physical structure and the performance of maternal functions place her at a disadvantage in the struggle for subsistence is obvious. This is especially true when the burdens of motherhood are upon her. Even when they are not, by abundant testimony of the medical fraternity continuance for a long time on her feet at work, repeating this from day to day, tends to injurious effects upon the body, and, as healthy mothers are essential to vigorous offspring, the physical well-being of woman becomes an object of public interest and care in order to preserve the strength and vigor of the race. . . .

Differentiated by these matters from the other sex, she is properly placed in a class by herself, and legislation designed for her protection may be sustained, even when like legislation is not necessary for men and could not be sustained. It is impossible to close one's eyes to the fact that she still looks to her brother and depends upon him. Even though all restrictions on political, personal, and contractual rights were taken away, and she stood, so far as statutes are concerned, upon an absolutely equal plane with him, it would still be true that she is so constituted that she will rest upon and look to him for protection; that her physical structure and a proper discharge of her maternal functions—having in view not merely her own health, but the well-being of the race—justify legislation to protect her from the greed as well as the passion of man. The limitations which this statute places upon her contractual powers, upon her right to agree with her employer as to the time she shall labor, are not imposed solely for her benefit, but also largely for the benefit of all. Many words cannot make this plainer. The two sexes differ in structure of body, in the functions to be performed by each, in the amount of physical strength, in the capacity for long-continued labor, particularly when done standing, the influence of vigorous health upon the future well-being of the race, the self-reliance which enables one to assert full rights, and in the capacity to maintain the struggle for subsistence. This difference justifies a difference in legislation, and upholds that which is designed to compensate for some of the burdens which rest upon her. . . .

For these reasons, and without questioning in any respect the decision in *Lochner* v. *New York,* we are of the opinion that it cannot be adjudged that the act in question is in conflict with the federal Constitution, so far as it respects the work of a female in a laundry, and the judgment of the supreme court of Oregon is

Affirmed.

Theodore Roosevelt on Conservation

December 3, 1907

This appeal in Roosevelt's Seventh Annual Message to Congress provides an ample statement in brief compass of his sense of the urgency of the conservation issue. It followed an aggressive policy of the sequestration of valuable governmental reserves and preceded a National Conservation Congress in 1908. The latter was attended by forty-four governors and many conservation experts, and it issued a strong statement favoring conservation policies. Soon afterward, forty-one states had conservation commissions of their own. H. R. Richardson, Messages and Papers of the Presidents *(New York ed., 1925) vol. XV, pp. 7094-99.*

. . . The conservation of our natural resources and their proper use constitute the fundamental problem which underlies almost every other problem of our National life. . . . As a nation we not only enjoy a wonderful measure of present prosperity but if this prosperity is used aright it is an earnest of future success such as no other nation will have. The reward of foresight for this Nation is great and easily foretold. But there must be the look ahead, there must be a realization of the fact that to waste, to destroy, our natural resources, to skin and exhaust the land instead of using it so as to increase its usefulness, will result in undermining in the days of our children the very prosperity which we ought by right to hand down to them amplified and developed. For the last few years, through several agencies, the Government has been endeavoring to get our people to look ahead and to substitute a planned and orderly development of our resources in place of a haphazard striving for immediate profit. Our great river systems should be developed as National water highways, the Mississippi with its tributaries, standing first in importance, and the Columbia second, although there are many others of importance on the Pacific, the Atlantic, and the Gulf slopes. The National Government should undertake this work, and I hope a beginning will be made in the present Congress; and the greatest of all our rivers, the Mississippi, should receive special attention. From the Great Lakes to the mouth of the Mississippi there should be a deep waterway, with deep waterways leading from it to the East and the West. Such a waterway would practically mean the extension of our coastline into the very heart of our country. It would be of incalculable benefit to our people. If begun at once it can be carried through in time appreciably to relieve the congestion of our great freight-carrying lines of railroads. The work should be systematically and continuously carried forward in accordance with some well-conceived plan. The main streams should be improved to the highest point of efficiency before the improvement of the branches is attempted; and the work should be kept free from every taint of recklessness or jobbery. The inland waterways which lie just back of the whole eastern and southern coasts should likewise be developed. Moreover, the development of our waterways involves many other important water problems, all of which should be considered as part of the same general scheme. The Government dams should be used to produce hundreds of thousands of horsepower as an incident to improving navigation; for the annual value of the unused water-power of the United States perhaps exceeds the annual value of the products of all our mines. As an incident to creating the deep waterways down the Mississippi, the Government should build along its whole lower length levees which, taken together with the control of the headwaters, will at once and forever put a complete stop to all threat of floods in the immensely fertile Delta region. The territory lying adjacent to the Mississippi along its lower course will thereby become one of the most prosperous and populous, as it already is one of the most fertile, farming regions in all the world. I have appointed an Inland Waterways Commission to study and outline a comprehensive scheme of development along all the lines indicated. Later I shall lay its report before the Congress.

Irrigation should be far more extensively developed than at present, not only in the States of the Great Plains and the Rocky Mountains, but in many others, as, for instance, in large portions of the South Atlantic and Gulf States, where it should go hand in hand with the reclamation of swampland. The Federal Government should seriously devote itself to this task, realizing that utilization of waterways and water-power, forestry, irrigation, and the reclamation of lands threatened with overflow, are all interdependent parts of the same problem. The work of the Reclamation Service in developing the larger opportunities of the western half of our country for irrigation is more important than almost any other movement. The constant purpose of the Government in connection with the Reclamation Service has been to use the water resources of the public lands for the ultimate greatest good of the greatest number; in other words, to put upon the land permanent home-makers, to use and develop it for themselves and for their children and children's children. . . .

The effort of the Government to deal with the public land has been based upon the same principle as that of the Reclamation Service. The land law system which was designed to meet the needs of the fertile and well-watered regions of the Middle West has largely broken down when applied to the drier regions of the Great Plains, the mountains, and much of the Pacific slope, where a farm of 160 acres is inadequate for self-support. . . . Three years ago a Public Lands commission was appointed to scrutinize the law, and defects, and recommend a remedy. Their examination specifically showed the existence of great fraud upon the public domain, and their recommendations for changes in the law were made with the design of conserving the natural resources of every part of the public lands by putting it to its best use. Especial attention was called to the prevention of settlement by the passage of great areas of public land into the hands of a few men, and to the enormous waste caused by unrestricted grazing upon the open range. The recommendations of the Public Lands Commission are sound, for they are especially in the interest of the actual home-maker; and where the small home-maker cannot at present utilize the land they provide that the Government shall keep control of it so that it may not be monopolized by a few men. The Congress has not yet acted upon these recommendations; but they are so just and proper, so essential to our National welfare, that I feel confident, if the Congress will take time to consider them, that they will ultimately be adopted.

Some such legislation as that proposed is essential in order to preserve the great stretches of public grazing land which are unfit for cultivation under present methods and are valuable only for the forage which they supply. These stretches amount in all to some 300,000,000 acres, and are open to the free grazing of cattle, sheep, horses, and goats, without restriction. Such a system, or lack of system, means that the range is not so much used as wasted by abuse. As the West settles, the range becomes more and more overgrazed. Much of it cannot be used to advantage unless it is fenced, for fencing is the only way by which to keep in check the owners of nomad flocks which roam hither and thither, utterly destroying the pastures and leaving a waste behind so that their presence is incompatible with the presence of home-makers. The existing fences are all illegal. . . . All these fences, those that are hurtful and those that are beneficial, are alike illegal and must come down. But it is an outrage that the law should necessitate such action on the part of the Administration. The unlawful fencing of public lands for private grazing must be stopped, but the necessity which occasioned it must be provided for. The Federal Government should have control of the range, whether by permit or lease, as local necessities may determine. Such control could secure the great benefit of legitimate fencing, while at the same time securing and promoting the settlement of the country. . . . The Government should part with its title only to the actual home-maker, not to the profit-maker who does not care to make a home. Our prime object is to secure the rights and guard the interests of the small ranchman, the man who ploughs and pitches hay for himself. It is this small ranchman, this actual settler and home-maker, who in the long run is most hurt by permitting thefts of the public land in whatever form.

Optimism is a good characteristic, but if carried to an excess it becomes foolishness. We are prone to speak of the resources of this country as inexhaustible; this is not so. The mineral wealth of the country, the coal, iron, oil, gas, and the like, does not reproduce itself, and therefore is certain to be exhausted ultimately; and wastefulness in dealing with it today means that our descendants will feel the exhaustion a generation or two before they otherwise would. But there are certain other forms of waste which could be entirely stopped—the waste of soil by washing, for instance, which is among the most dangerous of all wastes now in progress in the United States, is easily preventable, so that this present enormous loss of fertility is entirely unnecessary. The preservation or replacement of the forests is one of the most important means of preventing this loss. We have made a beginning in forest preservation, but . . . so rapid has been the rate of exhaustion of timber in the United States in the past, and so rapidly is the remainder being exhausted, that the country is unquestionably on the verge of a timber famine which will be felt in every household in the land. . . . The present annual consumption of lumber is certainly three times as great as the annual growth; and if the consumption and growth continue unchanged, practically all our lumber will be exhausted in another generation, while long before the limit to complete exhaustion is reached the growing scarcity will make itself felt in many blighting ways upon our National welfare. About twenty per cent of our forested territory is now reserved in National forests; but these do not include the most valuable timberlands, and in any event the proportion is too small to expect that the reserves can accomplish more than a mitigation of the trouble which is ahead for the nation. . . . We should acquire in the Appalachian and White Mountain regions all the forest lands that it is possible to acquire for the use of the Nation. These lands, because they form a National asset, are as emphatically national as the rivers which they feed, and which flow through so many States before they reach the ocean. . . .

Edward A. Ross on
The Criminaloid Type
1907

Edward A. Ross, the vigorous professor of sociology at the University of Wisconsin and one of the former advisers of Governor La Follette's regime (Doc. 23), was among the foremost academic thinkers who participated heartily in the Progressive movement. In his book, Sin and Society, *from which this passage is excerpted, he tried to make it clear that old conceptions of morals were not adequate for a sound system of social morality that recognized the realities of industrialism and an impersonal society. Old sins were still condemned, but new ones, in many ways more important because they were more far-reaching, were ignored. "You show," wrote Theodore Roosevelt to Ross, "that the worst evils we have to combat have inevitably evolved along with the evolution of society itself, and that the perspective of conduct must change from age to age. . . ."* Sin and Society *(Boston, 1907), pp. 46-57, 59-66.*

The real weakness in the moral position of Americans is not their attitude toward the plain criminal, but their attitude toward the quasi-criminal. The shocking leniency of the public in judging conspicuous persons who have thriven by antisocial practices is not due, as many imagine, to sycophancy. Let a prominent man commit some offense in bad odor and the multitude flings its stones with a right good will. The social lynching of the self-made magnate who put away his faded, toil-worn wife for the sake of a soubrette, proves that the props of the old morality have not rotted through. Sex righteousness continues to be thus stiffly upheld simply because man has not been inventing new ways of wronging woman. So long ago were sex sins recognized and branded that the public, feeling sure of itself, lays on with promptness and emphasis. The slowness of this same public in lashing other kinds of transgression betrays, not sycophancy or unthinking admiration of success, but perplexity. The prosperous evil-doers that bask undisturbed in popular favor have been careful to shun—or seem to shun—the familiar types of wickedness. Overlooked in Bible and Prayer-book, their obliquities lack the brimstone smell. Surpass as their misdeeds may in meanness and cruelty, there has not yet been time enough to store up strong emotion about

73

them; and so the sight of them does not let loose the flood of wrath and abhorrence that rushes down upon the long-attainted sins.

The immunity enjoyed by the perpetrator of new sins has brought into being a class for which we may coin the term *criminaloid*. By this we designate such as prosper by flagitious practices which have not yet come under the effective ban of public opinion. Often, indeed, they are guilty in the eyes of the law; but since they are not culpable in the eyes of the public and in their own eyes, their spiritual attitude is not that of the criminal. The lawmaker may make their misdeeds crimes, but, so long as morality stands stock-still in the old tracks, they escape both punishment and ignominy. Unlike their low-browed cousins, they occupy the cabin rather than the steerage of society. Relentless pursuit hems in the criminals, narrows their range of success, denies them influence. The criminaloids, on the other hand, encounter but feeble opposition, and, since their practices are often more lucrative than the authentic crimes, they distance their more scrupulous rivals in business and politics and reap an uncommon worldly prosperity.

Of greater moment is the fact that the criminaloids lower the tone of the community. The criminal slinks in the shadow, menacing our purses but not our ideals; the criminaloid, however, does not belong to the half world. Fortified by his connections with "legitimate business," "the regular party organization," perhaps with orthodoxy and the *bon ton,* he may even bestride his community like a Colossus. In his sight *and in their own sight* the old-style, square-dealing sort are as grasshoppers. Do we not hail him as "a man who does things," make him director of our banks and railroads, trustee of our hospitals and libraries? When Prince Henry visits us, do we not put him on the reception committee? He has far more initial weight in the community than has the clergyman, editor, or prosecutor who arraigns him. From his example and his excuses spreads an influence that tarnishes the ideals of ingenuous youth on the threshold of active life. . . .

THE KEY TO THE CRIMINALOID IS NOT EVIL IMPULSE BUT MORAL INSENSIBILITY

The director who speculates in the securities of his corporation, the banker who lends his depositors' money to himself under divers corporate aliases, the railroad official who grants a secret rebate for his private graft, the builder who hires walking delegates to harass his rivals with causeless strikes, the labor leader who instigates a strike in order to be paid for calling it off, the publisher who bribes his text-books into the schools, these reveal in their faces nothing of wolf or vulture. Nature has not foredoomed them to evil by a double dose of lust, cruelty, malice, greed, or jealousy. They are not degenerates tormented by monstrous cravings. They want nothing more than we all want—money, power, consideration—in a word, success; but they are in a hurry and they are not particular as to the means.

The criminaloid prefers to prey on the anonymous public. He is touchy about the individual victim, and, if faced down, will even make him reparation out of the plunder gathered at longer range. Too squeamish and too prudent to practice treachery, brutality, and violence himself, he takes care to work through middlemen. Conscious of the antipodal difference between doing wrong and getting it done, he places out his dirty work. With a string of intermediaries between himself and the toughs who slug voters at the polls, or the gang of navvies who break other navvies' heads with shovels on behalf of his electric line, he is able to keep his hands sweet and his boots clean. Thus he becomes a consumer of custom-made crime, a client of criminals, oftener a maker of criminals by persuading or requiring his subordinates to break law. Of course he must have "responsible" agents as valves to check the return flow of guilt from such proceedings. He shows them the goal, provides the money, insists on "results," but vehemently declines to know the foul methods by which alone his understrappers can get these "results." Not to bribe, but to employ and finance the briber; not to lie, but to admit to your editorial columns "paying matter"; not to commit perjury, but to hire men to homestead and make over to you claims they have sworn were entered in good faith and without collusion; not to cheat, but to promise a "rake-off" to a mysterious go-between in case your just assessment is cut down; not to rob on the highway, but to make the carrier pay you a rebate on your rival's shipments; not to shed innocent blood, but to bribe inspectors to overlook your neglect to install safety appliances: such are the ways of the criminaloid. He is a buyer rather than a practitioner of sin, and his middlemen spare him unpleasant details.

Secure in his quilted armor of lawyer-spun sophistries, the criminaloid promulgates an ethics which the public hails as a disinterested contribution to the philosophy of conduct. He invokes a pseudo-Darwinism to sanction the revival of outlawed and by-gone tactics of struggle. Ideals of fellowship and peace are "unscientific." To win the game with the aid of a sleeveful of aces proves one's fitness to survive. . . .

THE CRIMINALOID IS NOT ANTI-SOCIAL BY NATURE

Nation-wide is the zone of devastation of the adulterator, the rebater, the commercial free-booter, the fraud promoter, the humbug healer, the law-defying monopolist. State-wide is the burnt district of the corrupt legislator, the corporation-owned judge, the venal inspector, the bought bank examiner, the mercenary editor. But draw near the sinner and he whitens. If his fellow men are wronged clear to his doorstep he is criminal, not criminaloid. For the latter loses his sinister look, even takes on a benign aspect, as you come close. Within his home town, his ward, his circle, he is perhaps a good man, if judged by the simple old-time tests. Very likely he keeps his marriage vows, pays his debts, "mixes" well, stands by his friends, and has a contracted kind of public spirit. He is ready enough to rescue imperiled babies, protect maidens, or help poor widows. He is unevenly moral: oak in the family and clan virtues, but basswood in commercial and civic ethics. In some relations he is more sympathetic and generous than his critics; and he resents with genuine feeling the scorn of men who happen to have specialized in other virtues than those that appeal to him. Perhaps his point of honor is to give bribes but not to take them; perhaps it is to "stay bought" or not to sell out to both sides at once.

The type is exemplified by the St. Louis boodler, who, after accepting $25,000 to vote against a certain franchise, was offered a larger sum to vote for it. He did so, but returned the first bribe. He was asked on the witness-stand why he had returned it. "Because it wasn't mine!" he exclaimed, flushing with anger. "I hadn't earned it."

Seeing that the conventional sins are mostly close-range inflictions, whereas the long-range sins, being recent in type, have not yet been branded, the criminaloid receives from his community the credit of the close-in good he does, but not the shame of the remote evil he works.

Sometimes it is *time* instead of *space* that divides him from his victims. It is tomorrow's morrow that will suffer from the patent soothing-syrup, the factory toil of infants, the grabbing of public lands, the butchery of forests, and the smuggling in of coolies. In such a case the short-sighted many exonerate him; only the far-sighted few mark him for what he is. Or it may be a social interval that leaves him his illusion of innocence. Like Robin Hood, the criminaloid spares his own sort and finds his quarry on another social plane. The labor grafter, the political "striker," and the blackmailing society editor prey upward; the franchise grabber, the fiduciary thief, and the frenzied financier prey downward. In either case the sinner moves in an atmosphere of friendly approval and can still any smart of conscience with the balm of good fellowship and adulation. . . .

THE CRIMINALOID PRACTICES A PROTECTIVE MIMICRY OF THE GOOD

Because so many good men are pious, the criminaloid covets a high seat in the synagogue as a valuable private asset. Accordingly he is often to be found in the assemblies of the faithful, zealously exhorting and bearing witness. Onward thought he must leave to honest men; his line is strict orthodoxy. The upright may fall slack in devout observances, but he cannot afford to neglect his church connection. He needs it in his business. Such simulation is easier because the godly are slow to drive out the open-handed sinner who eschews the conventional sins. Many deprecate prying into the methods of any brother "having money or goods ostensibly his own or under a title not disapproved by the proper tribunals." They have, indeed, much warrant for insisting that the saving of souls rather than the salvation of society is the true mission of the church. . . .

Likewise the criminaloid counterfeits the good citizen. He takes care to meet all the conventional tests—flag worship, old-soldier sentiment, observance of all the national holidays, perfervid patriotism, party regularity and support. Full well he knows that the giving of a fountain or a park, the establishing of a college chair on the Neolithic drama or the elegiac poetry of the Chaldæans, will more than outweigh the dodging of taxes, the grabbing of streets, and the corrupting of city councils. Let him have his way about charters and franchises, and he zealously supports that "good government" which consists in sweeping the streets, holding down the "lid," and keeping taxes low. Nor will he fail in that scrupulous correctness of private and domestic life which confers respectability. In politics, to be sure, it is often necessary to play the "good fellow"; but in business and finance a studious conformity to the *convenances* is of the highest importance. The criminaloid must perforce seem sober and chaste, "a good husband and a kind father." If in this respect he offend, his hour of need will find him without support, and some callow reporter or district attorney will bowl him over like any vulgar criminal.

The criminaloid therefore puts on the whole armor of the good. He stands having his loins girt about with religiosity and having on the breastplate of respectability. . . .

THE CRIMINALOID PLAYS THE SUPPORT OF HIS LOCAL OR
SPECIAL GROUP AGAINST THE LARGER SOCIETY

The plain criminal can do himself no good by appealing to his "Mol lies," "Larrikins," or "Mafiosi," for they have no social standing. The criminaloid, however, identifies himself with some legitimate group, and when arraigned he calls upon his group to protect its own. The politically influential Western land thieves stir up the slumbering local feeling against the "impertinent meddlers" of the forestry service and the land office. Safe behind the judicial dictum that "bribery is merely a conventional crime," the boodlers denounce their indicter as "blackening the fair fame" of his state, and cry "Stand up for the grand old commonwealth of Nemaha!" The city boss harps artfully on the chord of local spirit and summons his bailiwick to rebuke the up-state reformers who would unhorse him. The law-breaking saloon-keeper rallies merchants with the cry that enforcement of the liquor laws "hurts business." The labor grafter represents his exposure as a capitalist plot and calls upon all Truss Riveters to "stand pat" and "vindicate" him with a reëlection. When a pious buccaneer is brought to bay, the Reverend Simon Magus thus sounds the denominational bugle: "Brother Barabbas is a loyal Newlight and a generous supporter of the Newlight Church. This vicious attack upon him is therefore a covert thrust at the Newlight body and ought to be resented by all the brethren." High finance, springing to the help of self-confessed thieves, meets an avenging public in this wise: "The Integrity Trust not only seeks with diabolical skill a reputation to blast, but, once blasted, it sinks into it wolfish fangs and gloats over the result of its fiendish act"; and adds, "This is not the true American spirit."

Here twangs the ultimate chord! For in criminaloid philosophy it is "un-American" to wrench patronage from the hands of spoilsmen, "un-American" to deal Federal justice to rascals of state eminence, "un-American" to pry into "private arrangements" between shipper and carrier, "un-American" to fry the truth out of reluctant magnates. . . .

Walter Rauschenbusch on
The Social Role of Christianity

1907

Walter Rauschenbusch had started his preaching career as a Baptist minister near the "Hell's Kitchen" slum of New York City, where, as he wrote, "one could hear human virtue cracking and crushing all around." The experience awakened him to the need for a social Christianity, and his new convictions were strengthened by further study and reflection in England and Germany. In 1897 he became a professor at the Rochester Theological Seminary, and it was from this vantage point that he wrote his Christianity and the Social Crisis, *one of the most influential statements of the new social Christianity, from which this passage is taken.* Christianity and the Social Crisis *(New York, 1907), pp. 367-72. Reprinted with the permission of The Macmillan Company.*

There are two great entities in human life—the human soul and the human race—and religion is to save both. The soul is to seek righteousness and eternal life; the race is to seek righteousness and the kingdom of God. The social preacher is apt to overlook the one. But the evangelical preacher has long overlooked the other. It is due to that protracted neglect that we are now deluged by the social problem in its present acute form. It is partly due to the same neglect that our churches are overwhelmingly feminine. Woman nurtures the individual in the home, and God has equipped her with an intuitive insight into the problems of the individual life. Man's life faces the outward world, and his instincts and interests lie that way. Hence men crowd where public questions get downright discussion. Our individualistic religion has helped to feminize our churches. A very protracted one-sidedness in preaching has to be balanced up, and if some now go to the other extreme, those who have created the situation hardly have the right to cast the first stone.

It seems likely that even after this present inequality of emphasis is balanced, some preachers will put more stress on the social aspects of religion. In that case we must apply Paul's large and tolerant principle, "There are diversities of gifts, but the same Spirit." Some by nature and training have the gift of dealing with individuals and the loving insight into personal needs; others have the passionate interest in the larger life and its laws. The Church needs evangelists and pastors, but it needs prophets too.

If a minister uses the great teaching powers of the pulpit sanely and wisely to open the minds of the people to the moral importance of the social questions, he may be of the utmost usefulness in the present crisis. Intelligent men who live in the midst of social problems do not yet know that there is a social problem, just as one may pass among the noises and sights of a city street without noticing them. If the minister can simply induce his more intelligent hearers to focus what is in their very field of vision, thereafter they cannot help seeing it, and information will begin to collect automatically in their minds. The Church itself has riveted the attention of the people on other aspects of life hitherto and thereby has diverted their attention from the social problems. It ought to make up for this.

A minister mingling with both classes can act as an interpreter to both. He can soften the increasing class hatred of the working class. He can infuse the spirit of moral enthusiasm into the economic struggle of the dispossessed and lift it to something more than a "stomach question." On the other hand, among the well-to-do, he can strengthen the consciousness that the working people have a real grievance and so increase the disposition to make concessions in practical cases and check the inclination to resort to force for the suppression of discontent. If the ministry would awaken among the wealthy a sense of social compunction and moral uneasiness, that alone might save our nation from a revolutionary explosion. It would be of the utmost importance to us all if the inevitable readjustment could be secured by a continuous succession of sensible demands on the one side and willing concessions on the other. We can see now that a little more wisdom and justice on both sides might have found a peaceable solution for the great social problem of slavery. Instead of that the country was plunged into the Civil War with its fearful cost in blood and wealth. We have been cursed for a generation with the legacy of sectional hatred, and the question of the status of the black race has not been solved even at such cost. If Pharaoh again hardens his heart, he will again have to weep for his first-born and be whelmed in the Red Sea. It is a question if we can rally enough moral insight and good-will to create a peaceable solution, or if the Bourbon spirit is to plunge our nation into a long-continued state of dissolution and anarchy which the mind shrinks from contemplating. The influence of the Christian ministry, if exercised in the spirit of Christian democracy, might be one of the most powerful solvents and the decisive influence for peace.

The spiritual force of Christianity should be turned against the materialism and mammonism of our industrial and social order.

If a man sacrifices his human dignity and self-respect to increase his income, or stunts his intellectual growth and his human affections to swell his bank account, he is to that extent serving mammon and denying God. Likewise if he uses up and injures the life of his fellow-men to make money for himself, he serves mammon and denies God. But our industrial order does both. It makes property the end, and man the means to produce it.

Man is treated as a *thing* to produce more things. Men are hired as hands and not as men. They are paid only enough to maintain their working capacity and not enough to develop their manhood. When their working force is exhausted, they are flung aside without consideration of their human needs. Jesus asked, "Is not a man more than a sheep?" Our industry says "No." It is careful of its live stock and machinery, and careless of its human working force. It keeps its electrical engines immaculate in burnished cleanliness and lets its human dynamos sicken in dirt. In the 15th Assembly District in New York City, between 10th and 11th Avenues, 1321 families in 1896 had three bathtubs between them. Our industrial establishments are institutions for the creation of dividends, and not for the fostering of human life. In all our public life the question of profit is put first. Pastor Stöcker, in a speech on child and female labor in the German Reichstag, said: "We have put the question the wrong way. We have asked: How much child and female labor does industry need in order to flourish, to pay dividends, and to sell goods abroad? Whereas we ought to have asked: How ought industry to be organized in order to protect and foster the family, the human individual, and the Christian life?" That simple reversal of the question marks the difference between the Christian conception of life and property and the mammonistic.

"Life is more than food and raiment." More, too, than the apparatus which makes food and raiment. What is all the machinery of our industrial organization worth if it does not make human life healthful and happy? But is it doing that? Men are first of all men, folks, members of our human family. To view them first of all as labor force is civilized barbarism. It is the attitude of the exploiter. Yet unconsciously we have all been taught to take that attitude and talk of men as if they were horse-powers or volts. Our commercialism has tainted our sense of fundamental human verities and values. We measure our national prosperity by pig-iron and steel instead of by the welfare of the people. In city affairs the property owners have more influence than the family owners. For instance, the pall of coal smoke hanging over our industrial cities is injurious to the eyes; it predisposes to diseases of the respiratory organs; it depresses the joy of living; it multiplies the labor of house-wives in cleaning and washing. But it continues because it would impose expense on business to install smoke consumers or pay skilled stokers. If an agitation is begun to abolish the smoke nuisance, the telling argu-ment is not that it inflicts injury on the mass of human life, but that the smoke "hurts business," and that it really "pays" to consume the wasted carbon. In political life one can constantly see the cause of hu-man life pleading long and vainly for redress, like the widow before the unjust judge. Then suddenly comes the bass voice of Property, and all men stand with hat in hand.

Our scientific political economy has long been an oracle of the false god. It has taught us to approach economic questions from the point of view of goods and not of man. It tells us how wealth is produced and divided and consumed by man, and not how man's life and develop-ment can best be fostered by material wealth. It is significant that the discussion of "Consumption" of wealth has been most neglected in po-litical economy; yet that is humanly the most important of all. Theology must become christocentric; political economy must become anthropo-centric. Man is Christianized when he puts God before self; political economy will be Christianized when it puts man before wealth. So-cialistic political economy does that. It is materialistic in its theory of human life and history, but it is humane in its aims, and to that extent is closer to Christianity than the orthodox science has been.

It is the function of religion to teach the individual to value his soul more than his body, and his moral integrity more than his income. In the same way it is the function of religion to teach society to value human life more than property, and to value property only in so far as it forms the material basis for the higher development of human life. When life and property are in apparent collision, life must take pre-cedence. This is not only Christian but prudent. When commercialism in its headlong greed deteriorates the mass of human life, it defeats its own covetousness by killing the goose that lays the golden egg. Hu-manity is that goose—in more senses than one. It takes faith in the moral law to believe that this penny-wise craft is really suicidal folly, and to assert that wealth which uses up the people paves the way to beggary. Religious men have been cowed by the prevailing materialism and arrogant selfishness of our business world. They should have the courage of religious faith and assert that "man liveth not by bread alone," but by doing the will of God, and that the life of a nation "consisteth not in the abundance of things" which it produces, but in the way men live justly with one another and humbly with their God.

Rheta Childe Dorr on
The Role of American Women
1910

Rheta Childe Dorr was a feminist who wrote regularly for the muckraking magazine Hampton's, *and who carried on investigations on women's work in factories and sweatshops somewhat like those of the Van Vorsts (Doc. 5). Her book,* What Eight Million Women Want, *from which this passage is taken, was made up chiefly from articles in* Hampton's. *With its assertion not only of the rights of women but of the special value of their role in reform, it struck a congenial note, and it sold a half million copies. Rheta Childe Dorr,* What Eight Million Women Want *(Boston, 1910), pp. 2-6, 11-13.*

Men, ardently, eternally, interested in Woman—one woman at a time —are almost never even faintly interested in women. Strangely, deliberately ignorant of women, they argue that their ignorance is justified by an innate unknowableness of the sex.

I am persuaded that the time is at hand when this sentimental, half contemptuous attitude of half the population towards the other half will have to be abandoned. I believe that the time has arrived when self-interest, if other motive be lacking, will compel society to examine the ideals of women. In support of this opinion I ask you to consider three facts, each one of which is so patent that it requires no argument.

The Census of 1900 reported nearly six million women in the United States engaged in wage earning outside their homes. Between 1890 and 1900 the number of women in industry increased faster than the number of men in industry. *It increased faster than the birth rate.* The number of women wage earners at the present date can only be estimated. Nine million would be a conservative guess. Nine million women who have forsaken the traditions of the hearth and are competing with men in the world of paid labor means that women are rapidly passing from the domestic control of their fathers and their husbands. Surely this is the most important economic fact in the world to-day.

Within the past twenty years no less than nine hundred and fifty-four thousand divorces have been granted in the United States. Two thirds of these divorces were granted to aggrieved wives. In spite of the anathemas of the church, in the face of tradition and early precept, in defiance of social ostracism, accepting, in the vast majority of cases, the responsibility of self-support, more than six hundred thousand women, in the short space of twenty years, repudiated the burden of uncongenial marriage. Without any doubt this is the most important social fact we have had to face since the slavery question was settled.

Not only in the United States, but in every constitutional country in the world the movement towards admitting women to full political equality with men is gathering strength. In half a dozen countries women are already completely enfranchised. In England the opposition is seeking terms of surrender. In the United States the stoutest enemy of the movement acknowledges that woman suffrage is ultimately inevitable. The voting strength of the world is about to be doubled, and the new element is absolutely an unknown quantity. Does anyone question that this is the most important political fact the modern world has ever faced?

I have asked you to consider three facts, but in reality they are but three manifestations of one fact, to my mind the most important human fact society has yet encountered. Women have ceased to exist as a subsidiary class in the community. They are no longer wholly dependent, economically, intellectually, and spiritually, on a ruling class of men. They look on life with the eyes of reasoning adults, where once they regarded it as trusting children. Women now form a new social group, separate, and to a degree homogeneous. Already they have evolved a group opinion and a group ideal.

And this brings me to my reason for believing that society will soon be compelled to make a serious survey of the opinions and ideals of women. As far as these have found collective expressions, it is evident that they differ very radically from accepted opinions and ideals of men. As a matter of fact, it is inevitable that this should be so. Back of the differences between the masculine and the feminine ideal lie centuries of different habits, different duties, different ambitions, different opportunities, different rewards.

I shall not here attempt to outline what the differences have been or why they have existed. Charlotte Perkins Gilman, in *Women and Economics,* did this before me—did it so well that it need never be done again. I merely wish to point out that different habits of action necessarily result, after long centuries, in different habits of thought. Men, accustomed to habits of strife, pursuit of material gains, immediate and tangible rewards, have come to believe that strife is not only inevitable but desirable; that material gain and visible reward are alone worth coveting. In this commercial age strife means business competition, reward means money. Man, in the aggregate, thinks in terms of money profit and money loss, and try as he will, he cannot yet think in any other terms. . . .

Women, since society became an organized body, have been engaged in the rearing, as well as the bearing of children. They have made the home, they have cared for the sick, ministered to the aged, and given to the poor. The universal destiny of the mass of women trained them to feed and clothe, to invent, manufacture, build, repair, contrive, conserve, economize. They lived lives of constant service, within the narrow confines of a home. Their labor was given to those they loved, and the reward they looked for was purely a spiritual reward.

A thousand generations of service, unpaid, loving, intimate, must have left the strongest kind of a mental habit in its wake. Women, when they emerged from the seclusion of their homes and began to mingle in the world procession, when they were thrown on their own financial responsibility, found themselves willy-nilly in the ranks of the producers, the wage earners; when the enlightenment of education was no longer denied them, when their responsibilities ceased to be entirely domestic and became somewhat social, when, in a word, women began to *think*, they naturally thought in human terms. They couldn't have thought otherwise if they had tried.

They might have learned, it is true. In certain circumstances women might have been persuaded to adopt the commercial habit of thought. But the circumstances were exactly propitious for the encouragement of the old-time woman habit of service. The modern thinking, planning, self-governing, educated woman came into a world which is losing faith in the commercial ideal, and is endeavoring to substitute in its place a social ideal. She came into a generation which is reaching passionate hands towards democracy. She became one with a nation which is weary of wars and hatreds, impatient with greed and privilege, sickened of poverty, disease, and social injustice. The modern, free-functioning woman accepted without the slightest difficulty these new ideals of democracy and social service. Where men could do little more than theorize in these matters, women were able easily and effectively to act.

I hope that I shall not be suspected of ascribing to women any ingrained or fundamental moral superiority to men. Women are not better than men. The mantle of moral superiority forced upon them as a substitute for intellectual equality they accepted, because they could not help themselves. They dropped it as soon as the substitute was no longer necessary.

That the mass of women are invariably found on the side of the new ideals is no evidence of their moral superiority to men; it is merely evidence of their intellectual youth.

Jane Addams Indicts
An Ancient Evil
1912

*When Jane Addams wrote this moving account of the circumstances
that impelled girls to take up prostitution, she had had almost a
quarter of a century of close observation of slum conditions, for her
social settlement, Hull House, had been opened in 1889. Her account
of this problem was one of the least sensational of the era, and one of
the most humane. Jane Addams,* A New Conscience and an Ancient
Evil *(New York, 1912), pp. 56-61, 89-94. Reprinted with the permission of The Macmillan Company.*

Successive reports of the United States census indicate that self-sup-
porting girls are increasing steadily in number each decade, until 59
per cent of all the young women in the nation between the ages of sixteen and twenty are engaged in some gainful occupation. Year after
year, as these figures increase, the public views them with complacency,
almost with pride, and confidently depends upon the inner restraint
and training of this girlish multitude to protect it from disaster. Nevertheless, the public is totally unable to determine at what moment these
safeguards, evolved under former industrial conditions, may reach a
breaking point, not because of economic freedom, but because of un-
toward economic conditions.

For the first time in history multitudes of women are laboring without the direct stimulus of family interest or affection, and they are also
unable to proportion their hours of work and intervals of rest according
to their strength; in addition to this, for thousands of them the effort
to obtain a livelihood fairly eclipses the very meaning of life itself. At
the present moment no student of modern industrial conditions can
possibly assert how far the superior chastity of woman, so rigidly maintained during the centuries, has been the result of her domestic surroundings, and certainly no one knows under what degree of economic
pressure the old restraints may give way.

In addition to the monotony of work and the long hours, the small
wages these girls receive have no relation to the standard of living which
they are endeavoring to maintain. Discouraged and over-fatigued, they
are often brought into sharp juxtaposition with the women who are
obtaining much larger returns from their illicit trade. Society also ven-

tures to capitalize a virtuous girl at much less than one who has yielded to temptation, and it may well hold itself responsible for the precarious position into which, year after year, a multitude of frail girls is placed

The very valuable report recently issued by the vice commission of Chicago leaves no room for doubt upon this point. The report estimates the yearly profit of this nefarious business as conducted in Chicago to be between fifteen and sixteen millions of dollars. Although these enormous profits largely accrue to the men who conduct the business side of prostitution, the report emphasizes the fact that the average girl earns very much more in such a life than she can hope to earn by any honest work. It points out that the capitalized value of the average working girl is six thousand dollars, as she ordinarily earns six dollars a week, which is three hundred dollars a year, or five per cent on that sum. A girl who sells drinks in a disreputable saloon, earning in commissions for herself twenty-one dollars a week, is capitalized at a value of twenty two thousand dollars. The report further estimates that the average girl who enters an illicit life under a protector or manager is able to earn twenty-five dollars a week, representing a capital of twenty-six thousand dollars. In other words, a girl in such a life "earns more than four times as much as she is worth as a factor in the social and industrial economy, where brains, intelligence, virtue and womanly charm should bring a premium." The argument is specious in that it does not record the economic value of the many later years in which the honest girl will live as wife and mother, in contrast to the premature death of the woman in the illicit trade, but the girl herself sees only the difference in the immediate earning possibilities in the two situations.

Nevertheless the supply of girls for the white slave traffic so far falls below the demand that large business enterprises have been developed throughout the world in order to secure a sufficient number of victims for this modern market. Over and over again in the criminal proceedings against the men engaged in this traffic, when questioned as to their motives, they have given the simple reply "that more girls are needed," and that they were "promised big money for them." Although economic pressure as a reason for entering an illicit life has thus been brought out in court by the evidence in a surprising number of cases, there is no doubt that it is often exaggerated; a girl always prefers to think that economic pressure is the reason for her downfall, even when the immediate causes have been her love of pleasure, her desire for finery, or the influence of evil companions. It is easy for her, as for all of us, to be deceived as to real motives. In addition to this the wretched girl

ho has entered upon an illicit life finds the experience so terrible that,
ay by day, she endeavors to justify herself with the excuse that the
ioney she earns is needed for the support of someone dependent upon
er, thus following habits established by generations of virtuous women
ho cared for feeble folk. I know one such girl living in a disreputable
ouse in Chicago who has adopted a delicate child afflicted with curva-
ire of the spine, whom she boards with respectable people and keeps
er many weeks out of each year in an expensive sanitarium that it
ay receive medical treatment. The mother of the child, an inmate
f the house in which the ardent foster-mother herself lives, is quite in-
fferent to the child's welfare and also rather amused at such solicitude.
he girl has persevered in her course for five years, never however al-
wing the little invalid to come to the house in which she and the
other live. The same sort of devotion and self-sacrifice is often poured
it upon the miserable man who in the beginning was responsible for
ie girl's entrance into the life and who constantly receives her earn-
gs. She supports him in the luxurious life he may be living in another
irt of the town, takes an almost maternal pride in his good clothes
id general prosperity, and regards him as the one person in all the
orld who understands her plight.

Most of the cases of economic responsibility, however, are not due to
iivalric devotion, but arise from a desire to fulfill family obligations
ich as would be accepted by any conscientious girl. This was clearly
vealed in conversations which were recently held with thirty-four girls,
ho were living at the same time in a rescue home, when twenty-two
 them gave economic pressure as the reason for choosing the life which
ey had so recently abandoned. One piteous little widow of seventeen
id been supporting her child and had been able to leave the life she
id been leading only because her married sister offered to take care of
e baby without the money formerly paid her. Another had been sup-
orting her mother and only since her recent death was the girl
re that she could live honestly because she had only herself to care
r. . . .

Difficult as is the position of the girl out of work when her family is
igent and uncomprehending, she has incomparably more protection
an the girl who is living in the city without home ties. Such girls
rm sixteen per cent of the working women of Chicago. With abso-
tely every penny of their meagre wages consumed in their inadequate
ring, they are totally unable to save money. That loneliness and de-
chment which the city tends to breed in its inhabitants is easily inten-

sified in such a girl into isolation and a desolating feeling of belongin
nowhere. All youth resents the sense of the enormity of the universe i
relation to the insignificance of the individual life, and youth, with tha
intense self-consciousness which makes each young person the very centr
of all emotional experience, broods over this as no older person ca
possibly do. At such moments a black oppression, the instinctive fea
of solitude, will send a lonely girl restlessly to walk the streets eve
when she is "too tired to stand," and when her desire for companior
ship in itself constitutes a grave danger. Such a girl living in a rente
room is usually without anyplace in which to properly receive caller
An investigation was recently made in Kansas City of 411 lodging-hous
in which young girls were living; less than 30 per cent were found wit
a parlor in which guests might be received. Many girls quite innocentl
permit young men to call upon them in their bedrooms, pitifully di
guised as "sitting-rooms," but the danger is obvious, and the standar
of the girl gradually become lowered.

Certainly during the trying times when a girl is out of work she shoul
have much more intelligent help than is at present extended to he
she should be able to avail herself of the state employment agenci
much more than is now possible, and the work of the newly establishe
vocational bureaus should be enormously extended.

When once we are in earnest about the abolition of the social evi
society will find that it must study industry from the point of view
the producer in a sense which has never been done before. Such a stud
with reference to industrial legislation will ally itself on one hand wit
the trade-union movement, which insists upon a living wage and short
hours for the workers, and also upon an opportunity for self-directio
and on the other hand with the efficiency movement, which would r
frain from over-fatiguing an operator as it would from over-speeding
machine. In addition to legislative enactment and the historic trad
union effort, the feebler and newer movement on the part of the er
ployers is being reinforced by the welfare secretary, who is not on
devising recreational and educational plans, but is placing before tl
employer much disturbing information upon the cost of living in r
lation to the pitiful wages of working girls. Certainly employers a
growing ashamed to use the worn-out, hypocritical pretence of emplo
ing only the girl "protected by home influences" as a device for reducir
wages. Help may also come from the consumers, for an increasing num
ber of them, with compunctions in regard to tempted young employee
are not only unwilling to purchase from the employer who underpa

his girls and thus to share his guilt, but are striving in divers ways to modify existing conditions.

As working women enter fresh fields of labor which ever open up anew as the old fields are submerged behind them, society must endeavor to speedily protect them by an amelioration of the economic conditions which are now so unnecessarily harsh and dangerous to health and morals. The world-wide movement for establishing governmental control of industrial conditions is especially concerned for working women. Fourteen of the European countries prohibit all night work for women and almost every civilized country in the world is considering the number of hours and the character of work in which women may be permitted to safely engage.

Although amelioration comes about so slowly that many young girls are sacrificed each year under conditions which could so easily and reasonably be changed, nevertheless it is apparently better to overcome the dangers in this new and freer life, which modern industry has opened to women, than it is to attempt to retreat into the domestic industry of the past; for all statistics of prostitution give the largest number of recruits for this life as coming from domestic service and the second largest number from girls who live at home with no definite occupation whatever. Therefore, although in the economic aspect of the social evil more than in any other do we find ground for despair, at the same time we discern, as nowhere else, the young girl's stubborn power of resistance. Nevertheless, the most superficial survey of her surroundings shows the necessity for ameliorating, as rapidly as possible, the harsh economic conditions which now environ her.

That steadily increasing function of the state by which it seeks to protect its workers from their own weakness and degradation, and insists that the livelihood of the manual laborer shall not be beaten down below the level of efficient citizenship, assumes new forms almost daily. From the human as well as the economic standpoint there is an obligation resting upon the state to discover how many victims of the white slave traffic are the result of social neglect, remedial incapacity, and the lack of industrial safeguards, and how far discontinuous employment and non-employment are factors in the breeding of discouragement and despair.

Is it because our modern industrialism is so new that we have been slow to connect it with the poverty and vice all about us? The socialists talk constantly of the relation of economic law to destitution and point out the connection between industrial maladjustment and individual wrongdoing, but certainly the study of social conditions, the obligatic to eradicate vice, cannot belong to one political party or to one ec nomic school. It must be recognized as a solemn obligation of existin governments, and society must realize that economic conditions can on be made more righteous and more human by the unceasing devotic of generations of men.

Walter Weyl on
The Revolt of the Consumer
1913

Walter Weyl was a magazine writer with a scholarly background. He had taken his Ph.D. at the University of Pennsylvania in 1897, and, after some years of travel and association with the labor movement, turned to magazine work. Of his first important work, The New Democracy, *from which this passage comes, he wrote: "It will be an argument for an American point of view in dealing with American conditions. It will be an argument for the Progressive Movement." Weyl was fascinated by the idea that the increasing wealth of the nation, far from discouraging discontent, had created a social surplus that gave the contending classes something to struggle for, and he believed that rising wealth was an aid to Progressive self-assertion. In this passage he analyzes the growing place of the consumer interest in the battle against the "plutocracy." Walter Weyl,* The New Democracy *(New York, 1913), pp. 249-54. Reprinted with the permission of The Macmillan Company.*

. . The plutocracy is more and more opposed by an ever larger number of social groups and individuals, not only for what it does and for what it is, but for the deeper economic tendencies which it represents. Different men are arrayed against the plutocracy for different reasons. While, however, such common hostility is a sufficient stimulus to an aggressive campaign, it is not a basis broad enough for a constructive program. Unless the opponents of the plutocracy have some common positive aim, their antagonism will dissipate itself in abortive assaults and waste heat, without permanent influence upon social conditions.

There exists, however, such a common aim. This aim, which holds together the opponents of an intrenched plutocracy, is the attainment of a common share in the conquered continent, in the material and moral accumulations of a century. When the trust raises prices, obtains valuable franchises or public lands, escapes taxation, secures bounties, lowers wages, evades factory laws, or makes other profitable maneuvers, it is diverting a part of the social surplus from the general community to itself. The public pays the higher prices, loses the franchises or lands, pays higher taxes, suffers in wages (and pays for the ill effects of low wages), and generally makes up dollar for dollar for all such gains. In all these things the people have a perceivable interest. The great mass i injured in its capacity of wage earner, salary earner, taxpayer, and consumer.

Of these capacities that of the consumer is the most universal, sinc even those who do not earn wages or pay direct taxes consume commodities. In America to-day the unifying economic force, about which majority, hostile to the plutocracy, is forming, is the common interest o the citizen as a consumer of wealth, and incidentally as an owner o (undivided) national possessions. The producer (who is only the consumer in another rôle) is highly differentiated. He is banker, lawyer soldier, tailor, farmer, shoeblack, messenger boy. He is capitalist, work man, money lender, money borrower, urban worker, rural worker. The consumer, on the other hand, is undifferentiated. All men, women, an children who buy shoes (except only the shoe manufacturer) are in terested in cheap good shoes. The consumers of most articles are over whelmingly superior in numbers to the producers.

Despite this overwhelming superiority in numbers, the consumer, find ing it difficult to organize, has often been worsted in industrial battle In our century-long tariff contests, a million inaudible consumers hav often counted less than has a petty industry in a remote district. Th consumer thought of himself as a producer, and he united only wit men of his own productive group. For a time there was a certain reaso for such an alignment. It was a period of falling prices, of severe com petition, in which the whole organization of industry favored the co sumer. In fact, the unorganized and ruthless consumer was blamed— and rightly blamed (as he is still rightly blamed to-day)—for many o the evils of industry. The curse of the sweat-shop and of the starvin seamstress, sewing by candle-light, was fairly brought to the doors of th bargain-hunting housewife. The consumer, though acting singly, fe himself secure.

Even when prices began to rise, consumers remained quiescent. Ther was greater difficulty in resisting price advances, because the loss to eac individual from each increase was so infinitesimal. The reverse of th overwhelming numbers of the consumers was the small individual in terest of each in each transaction. Wages affected a man far more sen sibly than did prices. If a motorman's wages were reduced one cent a hour he might lose thirty dollars a year; a rise of ten cents in the pric of shoes, on the other hand, meant a loss of, at most, two dollars a yea A man could not spend his lifetime fighting ten-cent increases. The cur for high prices was high wages.

As prices continue to rise, however, as a result (among other causes of our gradually entering into a monopoly period, a new insistence is laid upon the rights of the consumer, and political unity is based upon him. Where formerly production seemed to be the sole governing economic fact of a man's life, to-day many producers have no direct interest in their product. It is a very attenuated interest which the Polish slag-worker has in the duty on steel billets, but the Polish slag-worker and the Boston salesgirl and the Oshkosh lawyer have a similar interest (and a common cause of discontent) as consumers of the national wealth. The universality of the rise of prices has begun to affect the consumer as though he were attacked by a million gnats. The chief offense of the trust becomes its capacity to injure the consumer. Therefore the consumer, disinterred from his grave, reappears in the political arena as the "common man," the "plain people," the "strap-hanger," "the man on the street," "the taxpayer," the "ultimate consumer." Men who voted as producers are now voting as consumers.

We are now beginning to appeal to the "ultimate consumer," the man who actually eats, wears, or uses the article. A generation ago we legislated for the penultimate shopkeeper, or the ante-penultimate manufacturer. Our contest for railroad rate regulation was formerly waged in the interest of the producer or shipper, and not primarily in the interest of the consumer. The rates in question were freight, not passenger, rates, and the great problem was not so much low freight rates (which more immediately benefited the consumer) as equal freight rates, in which the competing manufacturer was primarily interested.

It is difficult for the consumer to act industrially in concert. The "rent strikes" on the East Side of New York have always been unsuccessful. The meat strikes have been equally without result. The work of the Consumers' Leagues has been chiefly a humanitarian labor for the benefit of producers, and we have never successfully developed in America great coöperative associations of workingmen consumers, like those of England, Belgium, France, and Germany. The appeal to the consumer has therefore been made on the political field.

To-day the consumer is represented on party platforms. It is in his interest that a "tariff revision downward" is demanded. Where one formerly heard in tariff discussions of the necessity of protecting the workingman from "the pauper labor of Europe," one now hears of the rights of the "ultimate consumer." Where, in discussions of land policy, one formerly heard of the need of giving the land to the actual settler (or producer), one now hears of preventing trusts from monopolizing mines, forests, and water sites, and thus raising the prices (to the consumer) of coal, wood, light, heat, and power. Our municipal ownership is in the interest of joint consumers, and more and more our railroad regulation is aiming at cheaper transportation.

To secure their rights as consumers, as well as to secure other economic interests, less in common, the people unite as citizens to obtain a sensitive popular government. They attain to a certain political as well as economic solidarity. This solidarity is by no means a complete unification of interest. There remain differences in agreement and discords in harmony. The middle classes are as much opposed to the trade-union as are the trusts, and the professional man is as anxious to secure a docile and cheap housemaid as the farmer is desirous of getting high prices for his wheat and paying low wages to his farm laborer.

The elements of solidarity, however, being found in a common hostility to the plutocracy and a common interest in the social surplus, it becomes possible gradually so to compromise conflicting interests within the group as to secure a united front against a common enemy. The regulation of railroads in the interest of consumer and farmer may be extended to the protection of the railroad worker; the conservation of natural resources may be linked to a similar policy of human conservation, to a campaign against destitution, and to a progressive labor policy which will insure the health, safety, comfort, and leisure of all workers. By such internal adjustments within the wide democratic army the possibility of a sufficient, permanent solidarity is given.

There is no evidence that the great army of potential democrats agree upon a clear-cut policy with regard to the solution of our economic problems. There is no reason to believe that they will ever agree in detail. But in various tentative and semiconscious ways they have already begun, through political organizations, non-political organizations, and through expressions of public opinion, to unite in formulating progressive plans. This coalescence is expressed in many ways, by a vote, by a storm of newspaper criticism, by the popularity of a democratic leader. This solidarity in formation does not express itself always on the same subject, nor does it always express itself consistently, but gradually it approves, one after another, a series of projects which, pieced together, constitute a democratic program. The fact that democracy, in so far as it has been hitherto approximated in America, has been attained not at one stroke, nor by one policy, but by a series of gradual and not always logical approaches, makes it appear possible that out of the great inchoate democratic mass of the community, with enlistments from below and with defections to the class above, will come the motive force to revolutionize society, to displace our present duality of resplendent plutocracy and crude ineffective democracy with a single, broad, intelligent, socialized, and victorious democracy.

Herbert Croly on
Unionism and the National Interest
1909

One of the things on which Progressives often disagreed was the proper place of labor unions in the national scheme of things. Most of them were altogether sympathetic to the situation of the working man, but many (Doc. 1) feared the power of union organization in much the same way as the power of the great corporations. Herbert Croly, who was one of these, expressed his concern in the following passage from The Promise of American Life. *A pronounced nationalist, and an advocate of strong leadership, Croly believed in pursuing progressive goals with firm Hamiltonian means, and his argument that the modern techniques of governmental organization must be accepted and vigorously used struck a note congenial to many intellectual Progressives. Among these was Theodore Roosevelt, whose later political principles (Doc. 24) were similar to Croly's, and who wrote him in 1910: "I do not know when I have read a book which I felt profited me as much as your book on American life. . . . I shall use your ideas freely in speeches I intend to make." Later, in 1914, Croly, joined by Walter Weyl (Doc. 18) and Walter Lippmann (Doc. 36), was the leading spirit in founding* The New Republic. *(See also Doc. 27.) Herbert Croly,* The Promise of American Life *(New York, 1909), pp. 127-31. Reprinted with the permission of The Macmillan Company.*

Some of the labor unions, like some of the corporations, have taken advantage of the infirmities of local and state governments to become arrogant and lawless. On the occasion of a great strike the strikers are often just as disorderly as they are permitted to be by the local police. When the police prevent them from resisting the employment of strike-breakers by force, they apparently believe that the political system of the country has been pressed into the service of their enemies; and they begin to wonder whether it will not be necessary for them to control such an inimical political organization. The average union laborer, even though he might hesitate himself to assault a "scab," warmly sympathizes with such assaults, and believes that in the existing state of industrial warfare they are morally justifiable. In these and in other respects he places his allegiance to his union and to his class above his allegiance to his state and to his country. He becomes in the interests of his organization a bad citizen, and at times an inhuman animal, who is ready to maim or even to kill another man and for the supposed benefit of himself and his fellows.

The most serious danger to the American democratic future which may issue from aggressive and unscrupulous unionism consists in the state of mind of which mob-violence is only one expression. The militant unionists are beginning to talk and believe as if they were at war with the existing social and political order—as if the American political system was as inimical to their interests as would be that of any European monarchy or aristocracy. . . .

Whether this aggressive unionism will ever become popular enough to endanger the foundations of the American political and social order, I shall not pretend to predict. The practical dangers resulting from it at any one time are largely neutralized by the mere size of the country and its extremely complicated social and industrial economy. The menace it contains to the nation as a whole can hardly become very critical as long as so large a proportion of the American voters are land-owning farmers. But while the general national well-being seems sufficiently protected for the present against the aggressive assertion of the class interests of the unionists, the local public interest of particular states and cities cannot be considered as anywhere near so secure; and in any event the existence of aggressive discontent on the part of the unionists must constitute a serious problem for the American legislator and statesman. . . .

The unionist leaders frequently offer verbal homage to the great American principle of equal rights, but what they really demand is the abandonment of that principle. What they want is an economic and political order which will discriminate in favor of union labor and against non-union labor; and they want it on the ground that the unions have proved to be the most effective agency on behalf of the economic and social amelioration of the wage-earner. The unions, that is, are helping most effectively to accomplish the task, traditionally attributed to the American democratic political system—the task of raising the general standard of living; and the unionists claim that they deserve on this ground recognition by the state and active encouragement. Obviously, however, such encouragement could not go very far without violating both the Federal and many state constitutions—the result being that there is a profound antagonism between our existing political system and what the unionists consider to be a perfectly fair demand. Like all good Americans, while verbally asking for nothing but equal rights, they interpret the phrase so that equal rights become equivalent to special rights.

Of all the hard blows which the course of American political and economic development has dealt the traditional system of political ideas and institutions, perhaps the hardest is this demand for discrimination on behalf of union labor. It means that the more intelligent and progressive American workingmen are coming to believe that the American political and economic organization does not sufficiently secure the material improvement of the wage-earner. This conviction may be to a large extent erroneous. Certain it is that the wages of unorganized farm laborers have been increasing as rapidly during the past thirty years as have the wages of the organized mechanics. But whether erroneous or not, it is widespread and deep-rooted; and whatever danger it possesses is derived from the fact that it affords to a substantially revolutionary purpose a large and increasing popular following. The other instances of organization for special purposes which have been remarked have superficially, at least, been making for conservatism. The millionaire and the professional politician want above all things to be let alone, and to be allowed to enjoy the benefit of their conquests. But the labor organizations cannot exercise the power necessary in their opinion to their interests without certain radical changes in the political and economic order; and inasmuch as their power is likely to increase rather than diminish, the American people are confronted with the prospect of persistent, unscrupulous, and increasing agitation on behalf of an economic and political reorganization in favor of one class of citizens.

The large corporations and the unions occupy in certain respects a similar relation to the American political system. Their advocates both believe in associated action for themselves and in competition for their adversaries. They both demand governmental protection and recognition, but resent the notion of efficient governmental regulation. They have both reached their existing power, partly because of the weakness of the state governments, to which they are legally subject, and they both are opposed to any interference by the Federal government—except exclusively on their own behalf. Yet they both have become so very powerful that they are frequently too strong for the state governments, and in different ways they both traffic for their own benefit with the politicians, who so often control those governments. Here, of course, the parallelism ends and the divergence begins. The corporations have apparently the best of the situation, because existing institutions are more favorable to the interests of the corporations than to the interests of the unionists; but on the other hand, the unions have the immense advantage of a great and increasing numerical strength. They are beginning to use the suffrage to promote a class interest, though how far they will travel on this perilous path remains doubtful. In any event, it is obvious that the development in this country of two such powerful and unscrupulous and well-organized special interests has created a condition which the founders of the Republic never anticipated, and which demands as a counterpoise a more effective body of national opinion, and a more powerful organization of the national interest.

Samuel Gompers Testifies on The Needs of Labor

1913

In striking contrast to the view of Croly (Doc. 19) is the direction of this argument by Samuel Gompers, president of the American Federation of Labor, and labor's most articulate spokesman. While labor leaders were pleased with gains made by the working class through social legislation, they regarded union organization, the wage bargain, and the strike as labor's surest protection. It had long rankled them that labor unions had been regarded by the courts as conspiracies in restraint of trade under the Sherman Act. When the following testimony was given before a Senate committee, Gompers himself was under a jail sentence (never served because of a Supreme Court ruling against the penalties) for activities held to be conspiratorial under the Sherman Act. The Clayton Act, which was the object of this testimony, never fulfilled Gompers's expectations, but in his crusade to lift the curse of court injunctions from the use of the strike as a weapon, he gave vent to many forthright expressions of the union point of view. Sixty-second Congress, Third Session, Senate Reports No. 1326 (Washington, 1913), Vol. II, p. 1728ff.

We are interested in securing relief from the interpretation placed upon the Sherman antitrust law by the Supreme Court of the United States, and the restoration of the working people, either as individuals or in association, to their status before the enactment of the law as interpreted by the court. In so far as the Sherman antitrust law is concerned, as now held as the law of the land, voluntary associations of the working people are regarded as combinations coming under the provisions of the anti-trust law and amenable to its civil and penal provisions. . . .

The Sherman antitrust law, as it has been interpreted, brings the men and women of labor under its civil and penal sections. As a consequence, any person or persons who may be injured in their business by reason of the normal and rightful action of working people, the person or persons so injured may bring suit and recover threefold damages. . . .

The men of labor want to know their status in society in the United States. They hold that their organizations are essential to their safety and well-being. It is not a matter of mere desire; nor are these organizations the growth of a desire on the part of those who are designated "labor leaders." Under modern industry there is no factor in all our governmental or civic life that undertakes to protect the working people against the power which wealth possesses in the hands of employers, corporations, combinations, and trusts of employers.

With the power of wealth and concentration of industry, the tremendous development in machinery, and power to drive machinery; with the improvement of the tools of labor, so that they are wonderfully tremendous machines, and with these all on the one hand; with labor, the workers, performing a given part of the whole product, probably an infinitesimal part, doing the thing a thousand or thousands of times over and over again in a day—labor divided and subdivided and specialized, so that a working man is but a mere cog in the great industrial modern plant; his individuality lost, alienated from the tools of labor; with concentration of wealth, concentration of industry, I wonder whether any of us can imagine what would be the actual condition of the working people of our country to-day without their organizations to protect them.

What would be the condition of the working men in our country in our day by acting as individuals with as great a concentrated wealth and industry on every hand? It is horrifying even to permit the imagination full swing to think what would be possible. Slavery! Slavery! Demoralized, degraded slavery. Nothing better.

To say that the men and women of labor may not do jointly what they may do in the exercise of their individual lawful right is an anomaly. . . .

Gentlemen, the individual working men accept conditions as they are, until driven to desperation. Then they throw down their tools and strike, without experience, without the knowledge of how best to conduct themselves, and to secure the relief which they need and demand. But the working men know where to go. It may be true that there are some workers who are opposed to organizations of labor, but they are very, very few. Those that do not come to us are either too helpless or too ignorant. But let no man fool himself. When in sheer desperation, driven to the last, where they can no longer submit to the lording of the master, they strike, they quit, and all the pent up anger gives vent in fury—they then come to us and ask us for our advice and our assistance, and we give it to them, whether they were indifferent to us or whether they were antagonistic to us. They are never questioned. We come to their assistance as best we can.

I do not pretend to say that with organizations of labor that strikes are entirely eliminated. I do not fool myself with any such beliefs, and I would not insult the intelligence of any other man by pretending to believe, much less to make, such a statement. But this one fact is sure: That in all the world there is now an unrest among the people, and primarily among the working people, with the present position they occupy in society—their unrequited toil; the attitude of irresponsibility of the employer toward the workers; the bitter antagonism to any effective attempt on the part of workers to protect themselves against aggression and greed, and the failure of employers to realize their responsibilities.

The demand of the workers is to be larger sharers in the product of their labor. In different countries they have unrest and this dissatisfaction takes on different forms. In our own country it takes on the form of the trade-union movement, as exemplified by the American Federation of Labor—a movement and a federation founded as a replica of the American governments, both the Federal Government and the State and city governments. It is formed to conform as nearly as it is possible to the American idea, and to have the crystallized unrest and discontent manifested under the Anglo-Saxon or American fashion; to press it home to the employers; to press it home to the lawmakers; to press it home to the law administrators, and possibly to impregnate and influence the minds of judges who may accord to us the rights which are essential to our well-being rather than guaranteeing to us the academic rights which are fruitless and which we do not want. . . .

PART THREE

Bossism and
Political Reform

William Allen White on
The Boss System
1910

William Allen White was in many ways one of the most representa-
tive minds produced by Middle Western Progressivism. In 1909 he
published a series of articles, collected the following year in his
book, The Old Order Changeth, *in which he described graphically*
the evils of the old boss system and the devices of democratic control
that he hoped would supplant it. "I worked hard on it," he later
wrote of his book, "and did what I thought was a research job writ-
ing to official sources in every state, getting a list of the new measures
passed there and really outlining definite trends." For about a decade
his book was widely used as a kind of standard text, a summation of
Progressive goals and achievements in this field. (See also Doc. 26.)
William Allen White, The Old Order Changeth *(New York, 1910),*
pp. 17-22, 29-31. Reprinted with the permission of William L. White.

Now it is not pleasant to recall American political conditions as they
were in the late nineties. Yet those conditions were founded so firmly on
local public sentiment and represented so thoroughly the judgment of
the average man, that—bad as they were—it becomes necessary to the
uses of this discussion to record them here briefly. For those conditions
furnish a starting point in the story of recent progress in this country
and only as we take a square look at the place where things were at their
worst, may we realize how much better they have grown.

Politics in America a dozen or fifteen years ago was founded upon the
boss system. At the bottom, in the smallest political unit, was the precinct
boss. Delegates to local party conventions were elected from precincts or
wards or townships.

The party convention in a county, town, or city was made up of from
two to four hundred of such delegates. They nominated the local county

township, ward, or city candidates for the offices that composed the local government. Generally county governments prevailed in rural communities in the West, in the Middle states, and in the South. The precinct boss at the bottom of the system generally said who should go to the county, town, or city convention as delegates. And in any precinct of two hundred votes or such a matter, not over fifty people in either party paid serious attention to politics. And year after year the same men represented each precinct in the local convention. They were the men who obeyed the dominant precinct boss at the base of things. He was not an officer of the government, but he controlled delegates to local conventions which nominated candidates for all the offices of the local government, so he became an actual part of the local government of every community. Half a dozen precinct bosses controlled the average county or small city. And the indomitable man among them controlled them.

This indomitable local boss had relations with the group of bosses that controlled the district or the great city. He was one of them. He controlled the larger group if he was strong enough. And he had relations with the still more powerful group of bosses that controlled the state conventions and state legislatures of his party. If he was one of the larger groups, he was powerful enough to say who should be nominated for the legislature in his county, who should have the judicial and congressional nominations in his district, and who should attend the state convention as delegates to name the candidates for state office. His nose was above water. He had a status in the politics of his state. He was someone. Sometimes he was a member of the actual organization of his party; at other times he preferred to name those who should be members. But always he controlled; and the fifty men in either party in each precinct who paid intelligent attention to politics, together with the fifty men in each of a score of other precincts in the town or city, knew this high-grade boss, went to him for favors, considered him as the vicegerent between them and the big boss who controlled the group of bosses in the inner temple that controlled the state.

The extra-constitutional place of the boss in government was as the extra-constitutional guardian of business. If a telephone company desired to put its poles in the street, and the city council objected, straightway went the owner of the telephone stock to the boss. He straightened matters out. If a street car company was having trouble with the city street department, the manager of the street railway went to the boss, and the street department became reasonable. If the water company was harassed by public litigation, the boss arranged a friendly suit to settle matters.

Always business was considered. And in some exceptional cases, vice was considered business. That was because vice paid rent, and property interests could not be disturbed. The boss, little or big, had the greatest respect for business, little or big. And this respect came to him not as a peculiar revelation—and perhaps not chiefly because business paid money to politics—but because he realized that all of the people about him felt as he felt. He merely reflected his environment. Otherwise more than fifty people would consider the little precinct boss obnoxious, and he would lose control, and a different group would conduct the public business of the precinct. So the secondary boss—the town or county boss —saw that local business was not hampered; and when the railroad company in the state desired to do as it pleased, the boss of the secondary bosses protected the railroad. And the people protected the bosses, and business big and little paid money into the party committees; and as the bosses controlled the committees the sale of special privilege was simple, legal, and unquestioned. Money in politics was there for the purpose of protecting the rights of property under the law, as against the rights of men. So prosperity dwelt among the people. The greed of capital was rampant, the force of democracy was dormant; "and the fool said in his heart there is no God."

But the folly grew national. Railroads, being the most important public service corporations in any state, had the closest relations with the state bosses who controlled members of the legislature, so the legal departments of the railroads named United States senators. In those days in many of the states a candidate for United States senator usually went to the law departments of the railroads in his state, and made his peace. Otherwise he was defeated. Now, man is a grateful brute, and when federal judges were to be named the law departments of the railroads generally had a judicial candidate in view. And the senator whose business it is to nominate federal judges for the President of the United States to appoint, subject to the Senate's confirmation, generally chose the man who was satisfactory to the powers in his state that made him senator. And as there are two sides to every lawsuit, whenever the interests of the public and the interests of the railroad clashed in court, it was as easy to see the railroad's side as it was to see the other side, so the mass of federal decisions for years favored the railroads. And thus the superficial government, in a most natural way, captured the Constitution. . . .

But now conditions are changing. Even when the knighthood of business was in flower there was the worm in the bud. There was the Spanish War. The spirit of sacrifice overcame the spirit of commercialism. Hanna lost control; the country declared war, and after waiting to prepare for

it as best he could McKinley proclaimed it. The retention of the Philip-
pines, which followed war, offended some of the quicker and more enlightened consciences of the people; but the crowd-conscience of the
nation saw with a deep subconscious wisdom of national genius that if
we could learn to sacrifice our own interest for those of a weaker people,
we would learn the lesson needed to solve the great problem of democracy—to check our national greed and to make business honest. For
business may not be made honest by vicarious sacrifice, but only as each
man is willing to sacrifice himself. The problem of democracy is at base
the problem of individual self-sacrifice coming from individual good will.
We cannot hope to socialize the forces of steam in our civilization until
we control and socialize ourselves.

And now for ten years there has been a distinct movement among the
American people—feeble and imperceptible against the current during
the first few years of its beginning—a movement which indicates that in
the soul of the people there is a conviction of their past unrighteousness.
During the recent years last past that movement has been unmistakable.
It is now one of the big self-evident things in our national life. It is
called variously: Reform, the Moral Awakening, the New Idea, the Square
Deal, the Uplift, Insurgency, and by other local cognomens; but it is one
current in the thought of the people. And the most hopeful sign of the
times lies in the fact that the current is almost world-wide. The same
striving to lift men to higher things, to fuller enjoyment of the fruits
of our civilization, to a wider participation in the blessings of modern
society—in short, to "a more abundant life"—the same striving is felt
through Europe and among the islands of the sea that is tightening the
muscles of our social and commercial and political body. And it may be
worth while to look about us and note the changes that are coming to
us in the days when they are in the making. For

> "The old order changeth, yielding place to new;
> And God fulfils himself in many ways,
> Lest one good custom should corrupt the world."

David Graham Phillips Attacks
A National Boss

April, 1906

For about two decades the Senate had been notorious as a citadel of special privilege when David Graham Phillips wrote his series of muckraking articles for the Cosmopolitan Magazine *on "The Treason of the Senate." Phillips, then thirty-nine, was a successful popular novelist, and he had little interest in undertaking the series proposed to him by the magazine's editor. But, provided with assistance in research, he consented, warmed to his task, and produced a sensational, declamatory series, which caused the* Cosmopolitan *to be sold out immediately on the newsstands and flooded with subscription orders. It was the appearance of this series, more than anything else, that inspired Theodore Roosevelt to attack the muckrakers (Doc. 2). Unlike many muckraking works, Phillips' was long on rhetoric and short on new facts. But few informed Progressives could doubt that the sketch of Senator Nelson W. Aldrich, excerpted here, was in general terms an accurate characterization of Aldrich's role as the center of a powerful bloc of conservative Senators who served great business interests. David Graham Phillips, "Aldrich, the Head of It All,"* Cosmopolitan Magazine, *April, 1906.*

He was born in 1841, is only sixty-four years old, good for another fifteen years, at least, in his present rugged health, before "the interests" will have to select another for his safe seat and treacherous task. He began as a grocery boy, got the beginning of one kind of education in the public schools and in an academy at East Greenwich, Rhode Island. He became clerk in a fish store in Providence, then clerk in a grocery, then bookkeeper, partner, and is still a wholesale grocer. He was elected to the legislature, applied himself so diligently to the work of getting his real education that he soon won the confidence of the boss, then Senator Anthony, and was sent to Congress, where he was Anthony's successor as boss and chief agent of the Rhode Island interests. He entered the United States Senate in 1881.

In 1901 his daughter married the only son and destined successor of John D. Rockefeller. Thus, the chief exploiter of the American people is closely allied by marriage with the chief schemer in the service of their exploiters. This fact no American should ever lose sight of. It is a political fact; it is an economic fact. It places the final and strongest seal upon the bonds uniting Aldrich and "the interests."

When Aldrich entered the Senate, twenty-five years ago, at the splendid full age of forty, the world was just beginning to feel the effects of the principles of concentration and combination, which were inexorably and permanently established with the discoveries in steam and electricity that make the whole human race more and more like one community of interdependent neighbors. It was a moment of opportunity, an unprecedented chance for Congress, especially its deliberate and supposedly sagacious senators, to "promote the general welfare" by giving those principles free and just play in securing the benefits of expanding prosperity to all, by seeing that the profits from the cooperation of all the people went *to* the people. Aldrich and the traitor Senate saw the opportunity. But they saw in it only a chance to enable a class to despoil the masses.

Before he reached the Senate, Aldrich had had fifteen years of training in how to legislate the proceeds of the labor of the many into the pockets of the few. He entered it as the representative of local interests engaged in robbing by means of slyly worded tariff schedules that changed protection against the foreigner into plunder of the native. His demonstrated excellent talents for sly, slippery work in legislative chambers and committee rooms and his security in his seat against popular revulsions and outbursts together marked him for the position of chief agent of the predatory band which was rapidly forming to take care of the prosperity of the American people. . . .

The sole source of Aldrich's power over the senators is "the interests" —the sole source, but quite sufficient to make him permanent and undisputed boss. Many of the senators, as we shall in due time and in detail note, are, like Depew and Platt, the direct agents of the various state or sectional subdivisions of "the interests," and these senators constitute about two-thirds of the entire Senate. Of the remainder several know that if they should oppose "the interests" they would lose their seats; several others are silent because they feel that to speak out would be useless; a few do speak out, but are careful not to infringe upon the rigid rule of "senatorial courtesy," which thus effectually protects the unblushing corruptionists, the obsequious servants of corruption, and likewise the many traitors to party as well as the people, from having disagreeable truths dinned into their ears. . . .

The greatest single hold of "the interests" is the fact that they are the "campaign contributors"—the men who supply the money for "keeping the party together," and for "getting out the vote." Did you ever think where the millions for watchers, spellbinders, halls, processions, posters, pamphlets, that are spent in national, state, and local campaigns come from? Who pays the big election expenses of your congressman, of the men you send to the legislature to elect senators? Do you imagine those who foot those huge bills are fools? Don't you know that they make sure of getting their money back, with interest, compound upon compound? Your candidates get most of the money for their campaigns from the party committees; and the central party committee is the national committee with which congressional and state and local committees are affiliated. The bulk of the money for the "political trust" comes from "the interests." "The interests" will give only to the "political trust." And that means Aldrich and his Democratic (!) lieutenant, Gorman of Maryland, leader of the minority in the Senate. Aldrich, then, is the head of the "political trust" and Gorman is his right-hand man. . . .

To relate the treason in detail would mean taking up bill after bill and going through it, line by line, word by word, and showing how this interpolation there or that excision yonder meant millions on millions more to this or that interest, millions on millions less for the people as merchants, wage or salary earners, consumers; how the killing of this measure meant immunity to looters all along the line; how the alteration of the wording of that other "trifling" resolution gave a quarter of a cent a pound on every one of hundreds of millions of pounds of some necessary of life to a certain small group of men; how this innocent looking little measure safeguarded the railway barons in looting the whole American people by excessive charges and rebates. Few among the masses have the patience to listen to these dull matters—and, so, "the interests" and their agents have prosperity and honor instead of justice and jail.

No railway legislation that was not either helpful to or harmless against "the interests"; no legislation on the subject of corporations that would interfere with "the interests," which use the corporate form to simplify and systematize their stealing; no legislation on the tariff question unless it secured to "the interests" full and free license to loot; no investigations of wholesale robbery or of any of the evils resulting from it—there you have in a few words the whole story of the Senate's treason under Aldrich's leadership, and of why property is concentrating in the hands of the few and the little children of the masses are being sent to toil in the darkness of mines, in the dreariness and unhealthfulness of factories instead of being sent to school; and why the great middle-class—the old-fashioned Americans, the people with the incomes of from two thousand to fifteen thousand a year—is being swiftly crushed into dependence and the repulsive miseries of "genteel poverty." The heavy and ever heavier taxes of "the interests" are swelling rents, swelling the prices of food, clothing, fuel, all the necessities and all the necessary comforts. And the Senate both forbids the lifting of those taxes and levies fresh taxes for its master. . . .

How does Aldrich work? Obviously, not much steering is necessary, when the time comes to vote. "The interests" have a majority and to spare. The only questions are such as permitting a senator to vote and at times to speak against "the interests" when the particular measure is mortally offensive to the people of his particular state or section. Those daily sham battles in the Senate! Those paradings of sham virtue! Is it not strange that the other senators, instead of merely busying themselves at writing letters or combing their whiskers, do not break into shouts of laughter?

Aldrich's real work—getting the wishes of his principals, directly or through their lawyers, and putting these wishes into proper form if they are orders for legislation or into the proper channels if they are orders to kill or emasculate legislation—this work is all done, of course, behind the scenes. When Aldrich is getting orders, there is of course never any witness. The second part of his task—execution—is in part a matter of whispering with his chief lieutenants, in part a matter of consultation in the secure secrecy of the Senate committee rooms. Aldrich is in person chairman of the chief Senate committee—finance. There he labors, assisted by Gorman, his right bower, who takes his place as chairman when the Democrats are in power; by Spooner, his left bower and public mouthpiece; by Allison, that Nestor of craft; by the Pennsylvania Railroad's Penrose; by Tom Platt of New York, corruptionist and lifelong agent of corruptionists; by Joe Bailey of Texas, and several other sympathetic or silent spirits. Together they concoct and sugar-coat the bitter doses for the people—the loot measures and suffocating of the measures in restraint of loot. In the unofficial but powerful steering committee—which receives from him the will of "the interests" and translates it into "party policy" —he works through Allison as chairman—but Allison's position is recognized as purely honorary.

And, also, Aldrich sits in the powerful interstate-commerce committee; there, he has his "pal," the brazen Elkins of West Virginia, as chairman. He is not on the committee on appropriations; but Allison is, is its chairman, and Cullom of Illinois is there—and in due time we shall endeavor to get better acquainted with both of them. In the commerce committee, he has Frye of Maine to look after such matters as the projected, often postponed, but never abandoned, loot through ship subsidy; in the Pacific Railroad committee he has the valiant soldier, the honest lumber and railway multi-millionaire, the embalmed-beef hero, Alger, as chairman;

in the post-office and post-roads committee, which looks after the rail-ways' postal graft, a clean steal from the Treasury of upward of ten millions a year—some put it as high as thirty millions—he has Penrose as chairman. In that highly important committee, the one on rules, he himself sits; but mouthpiece Spooner is naturally chairman. Their associates are Elkins and Lodge—another pair that need to be better known to the American people. Bailey is the chief "Democratic" member. What a sardonic jest to speak of these men as Republicans and Democrats! . . .

Such is Aldrich, the senator. At the second session of the last Congress his main achievements, so far as the surface shows, were smothering all inquiry into the tariff and the freight-rate robberies, helping Elkins and the group of traitors in the service of the thieves who control the railway corporations to emasculate railway legislation, helping Allison and Bailey to smother the bill against the food poisoners for dividends. During the past winter he has been concentrating on the "defense of the railways" —which means not the railways nor yet the railway corporations, but simply the Rockefeller-Morgan looting of the people by means of their control of the corporations that own the railways.

Has Aldrich intellect? Perhaps. But he does not show it. He has never in his twenty-five years of service in the Senate introduced or advocated a measure that shows any conception of life above what might be expected in a Hungry Joe. No, intellect is not the characteristic of Aldrich —or of any of these traitors, or of the men they serve. A scurvy lot they are, are they not, with their smirking and cringing and voluble palaver about God and patriotism and their eager offerings of endowments for hospitals and colleges whenever the American people so much as looks hard in their direction!

Aldrich is rich and powerful. Treachery has brought him wealth and rank, if not honor, of a certain sort. He must laugh at us, grown-up fools, permitting a handful to bind the might of our eighty millions and to set us all to work for them.

Lincoln Steffens Reports
La Follette's Reforms
1906

None of the reform governors enjoyed so broad a national reputation among Progressives as La Follette, who climaxed a long campaign for state reform in his election as governor of Wisconsin in 1900. Twice re-elected, La Follette resigned in 1905 to become United States Senator and to carry his reforming zeal into national affairs (See Doc. 30). The brilliant journalist Lincoln Steffens here recounts La Follette's struggles and achievements in Wisconsin. When Steffens first went to Wisconsin, he later wrote, it was in the conviction that La Follette was "a charlatan and a crook." But intensive investigation led him to the conclusion that La Follette was an example of "the heroism it takes to fight in America for American ideals." Lincoln Steffens, The Struggle for Self-Government *(New York, 1906), pp. 99-106, 108-19.*

"They" say in Wisconsin that La Follette is a demagogue, and if it is demagogy to go thus straight to the voters, then "they" are right. But then Folk also is a demagogue, and so are all thorough-going reformers. La Follette from the beginning has asked, not the bosses, but the people for what he wanted, and after 1894 he simply broadened his field and redoubled his efforts. He circularized the State, he made speeches every chance he got, and if the test of demagogy is the tone and style of a man's speeches, La Follette is the opposite of a demagogue. Capable of fierce invective, his oratory is impersonal; passionate and emotional himself, his speeches are temperate. Some of them are so loaded with facts and such closely knit arguments that they demand careful reading, and their effect is traced to his delivery, which is forceful, emphatic, and fascinating. . . .

What were the methods of the Sawyer-Payne-Spooner Republicans? [1] In

---

[1] Some of the main actors in Steffens' story require identification. During the 1890's, the Republican organization in Wisconsin underwent a split between the dominant Stalwart faction and La Follette's Halfbreeds. The leaders of the Stalwarts were Henry C. Payne, a railroad and utility magnate of great influence in both state and national Republican councils; the millionaire lumberman, Philetus Sawyer, who had served in the Senate from 1881 to 1893; and the railroad lawyer and corporation lobbyist, John C. Spooner (see Doc. 22), a Senator from 1885 to 1891 and from 1897 to 1907. La Follette's feud with the dominant Republicans broke out in the campaign of 1890, when he was abandoned by the machine leaders, and quickened in 1891, when he

1896 the next Governor of Wisconsin had to be chosen. The Stalwarts could not run Governor Upham again. As often happens to "safe men," the System had used him up; his appointments had built up the machine, his approval had sealed the compromise of the treasury cases. Someone else must run. To pick out his successor, the Stalwart leaders held a meeting at St. Louis, where they were attending a national convention, and they chose for Governor Edward W. Scofield. There was no demagogy about that.

La Follette wished to run himself; he hoped to run and win while Sawyer lived, and he was holding meetings, too. But his meetings were all over the State, with voters and delegates, and he was making headway. Lest he might fall short, however, La Follette made a political bargain. He confesses it, and calls it a political sin, but he thinks the retribution which came swift and hard was expiation. He made a deal with Emil Baensch, by which both should canvass the State for delegates, with the understanding that whichever of the two should develop the greater strength was to have both delegations. La Follette says he came into convention with enough delegates of his own to nominate him, and Baensch had seventy-five or so besides. The convention adjourned over night without nominating and the next morning La Follette was beaten. He had lost some of his own delegates, and Baensch's went to Scofield.

La Follette's lost delegates were bought. How the Baensch delegates were secured, I don't know, but Baensch was not a man to sell for money. It was reported to La Follette during the night that Baensch was going over, and La Follette wrestled with and thought he had won him back, till the morning balloting showed. As for the rest, the facts are ample to make plain the methods of the old ring. Sawyer was there; and there was a "barrel." I saw men who saw money on a table in the room in the Pfister Hotel, where delegates went in and out, and newspapermen present at the time told me the story in great detail. . . . The Half-breed leaders tried to catch the bribers with witnesses, but failed, and at midnight Charles F. Pfister, a Milwaukee Stalwart leader, called on La Follette, who repeated to me what he said:

---

accused Sawyer of attempting to bribe him. For the rest of the decade La Follette, along with such allies as Nils P. Haugen, a Scandinavian Congressman, and Isaac Stephenson, a wealthy and independent lumberman, struggled to unseat the Stalwarts from the governorship. In 1894, Haugen, backed by La Follette, lost the Republican nomination to W. H. Upham. In 1896, La Follette lost, under suspicious circumstances here recounted, some delegates he thought were his, and was defeated by the Stalwart candidate, Edward S. Scofield. In 1898 he was beaten again, but finally in 1900, as Steffens here explains, he won the nomination and election that led to a reform regime in Wisconsin.

"La Follette, we've got you beaten. We've got your delegates. It won't o you any good to squeal, and if you'll behave yourself we'll take care f you."

So La Follette had to go on with his fight. He would not "behave." His followers wanted him to lead an independent movement for Governor; he wouldn't do that, but he made up his mind to lead a movement or reform within the party, and his experience with corrupt delegates set him to thinking about methods of nomination. The System loomed large with the growth of corporate wealth, the power of huge consolidations over the individual, and the unscrupulous use of both money and power. Democracy was passing, and yet the people were sound. Their delegates at home were representatives, but shipped on passes to Milwaukee, treated, "entertained," and bribed, they ceased to represent. The most important reform was to get the nomination back among the voters themselves. Thus La Follette, out of his own experience, took up this issue—direct primary nominations by the Australian ballot.

During the next two years La Follette made a propaganda with this issue and railroad taxation, the taxation of other corporations—express and sleeping car companies which paid nothing—and the evils of a corrupt machine that stood for corrupting capital. He sent out circulars and literature, some of it the careful writings of scientific authors, but, most effective of all, were the speeches he made at the county fairs. When the time for the next Republican State convention came around in 1898, he held a conference with some thirty of his leaders in Milwaukee, and he urged a campaign for their platform alone, with no candidate. The others insisted that La Follette run, and they were right in principle. As the event proved, the Stalwarts were not afraid of a platform, if they could be in office to make and carry out the laws. La Follette ran for the nomination and was beaten—by the same methods that were employed against him in '96; cost (insider's estimate), $8,000. Scofield was renominated.

But the La Follette-Hall platform was adopted—anti-pass, corporation taxation, primary election reform, and all. "They" say now in Wisconsin that La Follette is too practical; that he has adopted machine methods, etc. During 1896, 1897, and 1898 they were saying he was an impracticable reformer, and yet here they were adopting his impracticable theories. And they enacted some of these reforms. The agitation (for La Follette is indeed an "agitator") made necessary some compliance with public demand and platform promises, so Hall got his anti-pass law at last; a commission to investigate taxation was appointed, and there was some other good legislation. Yet, as Mr. Hall said, "In effect, that platform was

repudiated." The railway commission reported that the larger companies
the Chicago, Milwaukee & St. Paul and the Northwestern, respectively
did not pay their proportionate share of the taxes, and a bill was intro
duced by Hall to raise their assessments. It passed the House, but th
Senate had and has a "combine" like the Senates of Missouri and Illinois
and the combine beat the bill.

The failures of the Legislature left all questions open, and La Follett
and his followers continued their agitation. Meanwhile Senator Sawye
died, and when the next gubernatorial election (1900) approached, al
hope of beating La Follette was gone. The Stalwarts began to come t
him with offers of support. One of the first to surrender was J. W. Bab
cock, Congressman and national politician. Others followed. . . . Thoug
the implacable Stalwarts supported the Democratic candidate, La Follett
was elected by 102,000 plurality.

Victory for reform is often defeat, and this triumph of La Follette, ap
parently so complete, was but the beginning of the greatest fight of al
in Wisconsin, the fight that is being waged out there now. Governor L
Follette was inaugurated January 7, 1901. The legislature was overwhelm
ingly Republican and apparently there was perfect harmony in the party
The Governor believed there was. The Stalwart-Halfbreed lines wer
not sharply drawn. The Halfbreeds counted a majority, especially in th
House, and A. R. Hall was the "logical" candidate for Speaker. It wa
understood that he coveted the honor, but he proposed and it was decide
that, in the interest of peace and fair play, a Stalwart should take th
chair. The Governor says that the first sign he had of trouble was in th
newspapers which, the day after the organization of the legislature, re
ported that the Stalwarts controlled and that there would be no primar
election or tax legislation. The Governor, undaunted, sent in a firn
message calling for the performance of all platform promises, and bill
to carry out these pledges were introduced under the direction of th
La Follette leaders, Hall and Judge E. Ray Stevens, the authority on th
primary election bill. These developed the opposition. There were tw
(alternative) railway tax bills; others to tax other corporations; and
later, a primary election bill—nothing that was not promised by a har
monious party, yet the outcry was startling and the fight that followe
was furious. Why?

I have seen enough of the System to believe that that is the way i
works. Just such opposition, with just such cries of "boss," "dictator,"
etc., arise against any Governors who try to govern in the interest of th
people. And I believe they will find their Legislatures organized an
corrupted against them. But in the case of La Follette there was a "mis

understanding." In the year (1900) when everything was La Follette, Congressman Babcock, Postmaster-General Payne, and others sought to bring together the great ruling special interests and the inevitable Governor. Governor La Follette said, like President Roosevelt, that he would represent the corporations of his State, just as he would represent all other interests and persons; but no more. He would be "fair." Well, that was "all we want," they said, and the way seemed smooth. . . . But after what I have seen in Chicago, St. Louis, and Pittsburgh, and in Missouri and Illinois and the United States, I almost am persuaded that no honest official in power can meet the expectations of great corporations; they have been spoiled, like bad American children, and are ever ready to resort to corruption and force. That was their recourse now.

Governor La Follette says he learned afterward that during the campaign, the old, corrupt ring went about in the legislative districts, picking and "fixing" legislators, and that the plan was to discredit him with defeat by organizing the Legislature against him. However this may be, it is certain that when his bills were under way, there was a rush to the lobby at Madison. The regular lobbyists were reinforced with special agents; local Stalwart leaders were sent for, and federal office-holders; United States Senators hurried home, and Congressmen; and boodle, federal patronage, force, and vice were employed to defeat bills promised in the platform. Here is a statement by Irvine L. Lenroot, now the Speaker of the Assembly. He says:

> From the first day of the session the railroad lobbyists were on the ground in force, offering courtesies and entertainments of various kinds to the members. Bribery is a hard word, a charge, which never should be made unless it can be substantiated. The writer has no personal knowledge of money being actually offered or received for votes against the bill. It was, however, generally understood in the Assembly that any member favoring the bill could better his financial condition if he was willing to vote against it. Members were approached by representatives of the companies and offered lucrative positions. This may not have been done with any idea of influencing votes.
>
> The reader will draw his own conclusions. It was a matter of common knowledge that railroad mileage could be procured if a member was "right." Railroad lands could be purchased very cheaply by members of the Legislature. It was said if a member would get into a poker game with a lobbyist, the member was sure to win. Members opposed to Governor La Follette were urged to vote against the bill, because he wanted it to pass. A prominent member stated that he did not dare to vote for the bill, because he was at the mercy of the railroad companies, and he was afraid they would ruin his business by advancing his rates, if he voted for it.

I went to Superior and saw Mr. Lenroot, and he told me that one of the "members approached by representatives of the companies and offered positions" was himself. He gave his bribery stories in detail, and enabled me to run down and verify others; but the sentence that interested me most in his statement was the last. The member who did not dare vote for the railway tax bill, lest the railways raise the freight on his goods and ruin his business, confessed to Governor La Follette and others. Another member stated that in return for his treason to his constituents, a railroad quoted him a rate that would give him an advantage over his competitors.

Well, these methods succeeded. The policy of the administration was not carried out. Some good bills passed, but the session was a failure. Not content with this triumph, however, the System went to work to beat La Follette, and to accomplish this end, La Follette's methods were adopted, or, rather, adapted. A systematic appeal was to be made to public opinion. . . .

These "democratic" methods failed. When the time arrived for the next Republican State convention, the Stalwarts found that the people had sent up delegates instructed for La Follette, and he was nominated for a second term. What could the Stalwarts do? They weren't even "regular" now. La Follette had the party, they had only the federal patronage and the Big Business System. But the System had resources. Wherever a municipal reform movement has hewed to the line, the leaders of it, like Folk and the Chicago reformers, have seen the force of corruption retire from one party to the other and from the city to the State. This Wisconsin movement for State reform now had a similar experience. The Wisconsin System, driven out of the Republican, went over to the Democratic party; that had not been reformed; beaten out of power in the State, it retreated to the towns; they had not been reformed.

The System in many of the Wisconsin municipalities was intact. There had been no serious municipal reform movements anywhere, and the citizens of Milwaukee, Oshkosh, Green Bay, etc., were pretty well satisfied, and they are still, apparently. "We're nothing like Minneapolis, St. Louis, and the rest," they told me with American complacency. Green Bay was exactly like Minneapolis; we know it because the wretched little place has been exposed since. . . .

District Attorney Bennett has had grand juries at work in Milwaukee since 1901, and he has some forty-two persons indicted—twelve aldermen, ten supervisors, nine other officials, one State Senator, and ten citizens; four convictions and three pleas of guilty. The grafting so far exposed is petty, but the evidence in hand indicates a highly perfected boodle system. The Republicans had the county, the Democrats the city, and both the council and the board of supervisors had combines which grafted on contracts, public institutions, franchises, and other business privileges. The corrupt connection of business and politics was shown; the informants were merchants and contractors, mostly small men, who confessed to bribery. The biggest caught so far is Colonel Pabst, the brewer, who paid a check of $1,500 for leave to break a building law. But all signs point higher than beer, to more "legitimate" political business. As in Chicago, a bank is the center of this graft (The First National Bank, the president of which is now in the penitentiary), and public utility companies are back of it. The politicians in the boards of management, now or formerly, show that. It is a bipartisan system all through. Henry C. Payne, while chairman of the Republican State Central Committee, and E. C. Wall (the man the Wisconsin Democracy offered to the National Democratic Convention for President of the United States), while chairman of the Democratic State Central Committee, engineered a consolidation of Milwaukee street railway and electric lighting companies, and, when the job was done, Payne became manager of the street railway, Wall of the light company. But this was "business." There was no scandal about it. The great scandal of Milwaukee was the extension of street railway franchises, and the men who put that through were Charles F. Pfister, the Stalwart Republican boss, and David S. Rose, the Stalwart Democratic Mayor. Money was paid; the extension was boodled through. The Milwaukee *Sentinel* reprinted a paragraph saying Pfister, among others, did the bribing, and thus it happened that the Stalwarts got that paper. Pfister sued for libel, but when the editors (now on the Milwaukee *Free Press*) made answer that their defense would be proof of the charge, the millionaire traction man bought the paper and its evidence, too. It is no more than fair to add—as Milwaukee newspapermen always do (with delight)—that the paper had very little evidence, not nearly so much as Pfister seemed to think it had. As for Mayor Rose, his friends declare that he has told them, personally and convincingly, that he got not one cent for his service. But that is not the point. Mayor Rose fought to secure for special interests a concession which sacrificed the common interests of his city. I am aware that he defends the terms of the grants as fair, and they would seem so in the East, but the West is intelligent on special privileges, and Mayor Rose lost to Milwaukee the chance Chicago seized to tackle the public utility problem. Moreover, Rose knew that his council was corrupt before it was proven so; he told two businessmen that they couldn't get a privilege they sought honestly from him without bribing aldermen. Yet he ridiculed as "hot air" an investigation which produced evidence enough to defeat at the polls, in a self-respecting city, the head of an administration so besmirched. Nevertheless, Milwaukee reëlected Rose; good citizens say that they gave the man the benefit of the doubt—the man, not the city.

But this is not the only explanation. The System was on trial with Mayor Rose in that election, and the System saved its own. The Republicans, with the Rose administration exposed, had a chance to win, and they nominated a good man, Mr. Guy D. Goff. Pfister, the Stalwart Republican boss, seemed to support Goff; certainly the young candidate had no suspicion to the contrary. He has now, however. When the returns came in showing that he was beaten, Mr. Goff hunted up Mr. Pfister, and he found him. Mr. Goff, the Republican candidate for Mayor, found Charles F. Pfister, the Stalwart Republican boss, rejoicing over the drinks with the elected Democratic Mayor, David S. Rose!

I guess Mr. Goff knows that a bipartisan System rules Milwaukee, and, by the same token, Governor La Follette knows that there is a bipartisan System in Wisconsin. For when Governor La Follette beat the Stalwarts in the Republican State convention of 1902, those same Stalwarts combined with the Democrats. Democrats told me that the Republican Stalwarts dictated the "Democratic" anti-La Follette platform, and that Pfister, the "Republican" boss, named the "safe man" chosen for the "Democratic" candidate for Governor to run against La Follette—said David S. Rose.

"They" say in Wisconsin that La Follette is a Democrat; that "he appeals to Democratic voters." He does. He admits it, but he adds that it is indeed to the Democratic voters that he appeals—not to the Democratic machine. And he gets Democratic votes. "They" complain that he has split the Republican party; he has, and he has split the Democratic party, too. When "they" united the two party rings of the bipartisan System against La Follette in 1902, he went out after the voters of both parties, and those voters combined; they beat Rose, the two rings, and the System. The people of Wisconsin reëlected La Follette, the "unsafe," and that is why the trouble is so great in Wisconsin. The System there is down.

There is a machine, but it is La Follette's. When he was reëlected, the Governor organized his party, and I think no other of his offenses is quite so heinous in Stalwart eyes. They wanted me to expose him as a boss who had used State patronage to build up an organization. I reminded "them" that their federal patronage is greater than La Follette's State patronage, and I explained that my prejudice was not against organization; their kind everywhere had been urging me so long to believe that organization was necessary in politics that I was disposed to denounce only those machines that sold out the party and the people. And as for the "boss"—it is not the boss in an elective office where he is responsible that is so bad, but the irresponsible boss back of a safe figurehead; this is the man that is really dangerous. They declared, however, that Governor La Follette had sacrificed good service to the upbuilding of his machine. This is a serious charge. I did not go thoroughly into it. Cases which I investigated at Stalwart behest, held, with one exception, very little water, and I put no faith in the rest. But, for the sake of argument, let us admit that the departments are not all that they should be. What then? As in Chicago, the fight in Wisconsin is for self-government, not "good" government; it is a fight to reëstablish a government representative of all the people. Given that; remove from control the Big Business and the Bad Politics that corrupt all branches of the government, and "good" government will come easily enough. But Big Business and Bad Politics are hard to beat.

The defeat of Rose did not beat them. The Stalwarts still had the Senate, and they manned the lobby to beat the railroad tax and the primary election bills. But Governor La Follette outplayed them at the great game. He long had been studying the scheme for a State commission to regulate railway freight rates. It was logical. If their taxes were increased the roads could take the difference out of the people by raising freight rates. Other States had such commissions, and in some of them, notably Iowa and Illinois, the rates were lower than in Wisconsin. Moreover, we all know railroads give secret rebates and otherwise discriminate in favor of individuals and localities.

When, then, the battle lines were drawn on the old bills in the Legislature of 1903, the Governor threw into the fight a bristling message calling for a commission to regulate railway rates. The effect was startling. "Populism!" "Socialism!" "they" cried, and they turned to rend this new bill. They let the tax bill go through to fight this fresh menace to "business." They held out against the primary election bill also, for if that passed they feared the people might keep La Follette in power forever. Even that, however, they let pass finally, with an amendment for a referendum. Concentrating upon the rate commission bill, Big Business organized businessmen's mass meetings throughout the State, and with the help of favored or timid shippers, sent committees to Madison to protest to the Legislature. Thus this bill in the interests of fair business was beaten by business, and, with the primary election referendum, is an issue in this year's campaign (1904).

As I have tried to show, however, the fundamental issue lies deeper. The people of Wisconsin understand this. The Stalwarts dread the test at the polls. But what other appeal was there? They knew one. When the Republican State convention met this year, the Stalwarts bolted; whatever the result might have been of a fight in the convention, they avoided it and held a separate convention in another hall, which, by the way, they had hired in advance. The Halfbreeds renominated La Follette; the Stalwarts put up another ticket. To the Stalwart convention came Post-master-General Payne, United States Senators Spooner and Quarles, Stalwart Congressmen, and federal officeholders—the Federal System. The broken State System was appealing to the United States System, and the Republican National Convention at Chicago was to decide the case. And it did decide—for the System. I attended that convention, and heard what was said privately and honestly. The Republicans who decided for Payne-Spooner-Pfister, Babcock, et al., said "La Follette isn't really a Republican anyhow."

Isn't he? That is a most important question. True, he is very demo-cratic essentially. He helped to draw the McKinley tariff law and he is standing now on the national Republican platform; his democracy con-sists only in the belief that the citizens elected to represent the people should represent the people, not the corrupt special interests. Both par-ties should be democratic in that sense. But they aren't. Too often we have found both parties representing graft—big business graft. The peo-ple, especially in the West, are waking to a realization of this state of things, and (taking a hint from the Big Grafters) they are following leaders who see that the way to restore government representative of the common interests of the city or State is to restore to public opinion the control of the dominant party. . . . The people of Wisconsin are not radi-cals; they are law-abiding, conservative, and fair. They will lay great store by what their courts shall rule, but this is a question that should be left wholly to the people themselves. And they are to be trusted, for no matter how men may differ about Governor La Follette otherwise, his long, hard fight has developed citizenship in Wisconsin—honest, rea-sonable, intelligent citizenship. And that is better than "business"; that is what business and government are for—men.

Theodore Roosevelt on
The New Nationalism
29 and 31 August, 1910

Upon his return in 1910 from a long trip abroad, the ex-President soon became discouraged with President Taft, and at last decided to strengthen the Progressive wing of the Republican party. In a series of speeches made during the late summer of 1910, he espoused some doctrines more radical than any he had endorsed during his presidency. In these speeches, he appealed in a Crolyesque fashion (Docs. 19 and 27) for what he called "The New Nationalism." Conservatives were particularly alarmed by his suggestion that the judiciary should "be interested primarily in human welfare rather than in property," but he was to go still further on this subject before the Progressive campaign of 1912. Two speeches are excerpted in these passages. Theodore Roosevelt, The New Nationalism (New York, 1910), pp. 11-14, 17-18, 28-30, 41-43. Also available in the Spectrum Classics in History Series.

I stand for the square deal. But when I say that I am for the square deal, I mean not merely that I stand for fair play under the present rules of the game, but that I stand for having those rules changed so as to work for a more substantial equality of opportunity and of reward for equally good service. One word of warning, which, I think, is hardly necessary in Kansas. When I say I want a square deal for the poor man, I do not mean that I want a square deal for the man who remains poor because he has not the energy to work for himself. If a man who has had a chance will not make good, then he has got to quit. And you men of the Grand Army, you want justice for the brave man who fought, and punishment for the coward who shirked his work. Is not that so?

Now, this means that our government, national and state, must be freed from the sinister influence or control of special interests. Exactly as the special interests of cotton and slavery threatened our political integrity before the Civil War, so now the great special business interests too often control and corrupt the men and methods of government for their own profit. We must drive the special interests out of politics. That is one of our tasks to-day. Every special interest is entitled to justice—full, fair, and complete,—and, now, mind you, if there were any attempt by mob violence to plunder and work harm to the special interest, what-

ever it may be, that I most dislike, and the wealthy man, whomsoev
he may be, for whom I have the greatest contempt, I would fight f
him, and you would if you were worth your salt. He should have justic
For every special interest is entitled to justice, but not one is entitled
a vote in Congress, to a voice on the bench, or to representation in ar
public office. The Constitution guarantees protection to property, an
we must make that promise good. But it does not give the right
suffrage to any corporation.

The true friend of property, the true conservative, is he who insis
that property shall be the servant and not the master of the commo
wealth; who insists that the creature of man's making shall be the serva
and not the master of the man who made it. The citizens of the Unite
States must effectively control the mighty commercial forces which th
have themselves called into being.

There can be no effective control of corporations while their politic
activity remains. To put an end to it will be neither a short nor an ea
task, but it can be done.

We must have complete and effective publicity of corporate affairs,
that the people may know beyond peradventure whether the corporatio
obey the law and whether their management entitles them to the co
fidence of the public. It is necessary that laws should be passed to pr
hibit the use of corporate funds directly or indirectly for politic
purposes; it is still more necessary that such laws should be thorough
enforced. Corporate expenditures for political purposes, and especial
such expenditures by public service corporations, have supplied one
the principal sources of corruption in our political affairs.

It has become entirely clear that we must have government supe
vision of the capitalization, not only of public service corporations, i
cluding, particularly, railways, but of all corporations doing an intersta
business. I do not wish to see the nation forced into the ownership
the railways if it can possibly be avoided, and the only alternative
thoroughgoing and effective regulation, which shall be based on a fu
knowledge of all the facts, including a physical valuation of propert
This physical valuation is not needed, or, at least, is very rarely neede
for fixing rates; but it is needed as the basis of honest capitalization. . .

The absence of effective state, and, especially, national, restraint up
unfair money getting has tended to create a small class of enormous
wealthy and economically powerful men, whose chief object is to ho
and increase their power. The prime need is to change the conditio
which enable these men to accumulate power which it is not for t
general welfare that they should hold or exercise. We grudge no man

fortune which represents his own power and sagacity, when exercised with entire regard to the welfare of his fellows. Again, comrades over there, take the lesson from your own experience. Not only did you not grudge, but you gloried in the promotion of the great generals who gained their promotion by leading the army to victory. So it is with us. We grudge no man a fortune in civil life if it is honorably obtained and well used. It is not even enough that it should have been gained without doing damage to the community. We should permit it to be gained only so long as the gaining represents benefit to the community. This, I know, implies a policy of a far more active governmental interference with social and economic conditions in this country than we have yet had, but I think we have got to face the fact that such an increase in governmental control is now necessary.

No man should receive a dollar unless that dollar has been fairly earned. Every dollar received should represent a dollar's worth of service rendered—not gambling in stocks, but service rendered. The really big fortune, the swollen fortune, by the mere fact of its size acquires qualities which differentiate it in kind as well as in degree from what is possessed by men of relatively small means. Therefore, I believe in a graduated income tax on big fortunes, and in another tax which is far more easily collected and far more effective—a graduated inheritance tax on big fortunes, properly safeguarded against evasion and increasing rapidly in amount with the size of the estate. . . .

The American people are right in demanding that New Nationalism, without which we cannot hope to deal with new problems. The New Nationalism puts the national need before sectional or personal advantage. It is impatient of the utter confusion that results from local legislatures attempting to treat national issues as local issues. It is still more impatient of the impotence which springs from overdivision of governmental powers, the impotence which makes it possible for local selfishness or for legal cunning, hired by wealthy special interests, to bring national activities to a deadlock. This New Nationalism regards the executive power as the steward of the public welfare. It demands of the judiciary that it shall be interested primarily in human welfare rather than in property, just as it demands that the representative body shall represent all the people rather than any one class or section of the people.

I believe in shaping the ends of government to protect property as well as human welfare. Normally, and in the long run, the ends are the same; but whenever the alternative must be faced, I am for men and not for property, as you were in the Civil War. I am far from underestimating the importance of dividends; but I rank dividends below human

character. Again, I do not have any sympathy with the reformer wh
says he does not care for dividends. Of course, economic welfare is nece
sary, for a man must pull his own weight and be able to support hi
family. I know well that the reformers must not bring upon the peopl
economic ruin, or the reforms themselves will go down in the ruin. Bu
we must be ready to face temporary disaster, whether or not brought o
by those who will war against us to the knife. Those who oppose a
reform will do well to remember that ruin in its worst form is inevitabl
if our national life brings us nothing better than swollen fortunes fo
the few and the triumph in both politics and business of a sordid an
selfish materialism.

If our political institutions were perfect, they would absolutely pr
vent the political domination of money in any part of our affairs. W
need to make our political representatives more quickly and sensitivel
responsive to the people whose servants they are. More direct action b
the people in their own affairs under proper safeguards is vitally nece
sary. The direct primary is a step in this direction, if it is associate
with a corrupt practices act effective to prevent the advantage of th
man willing recklessly and unscrupulously to spend money over his mor
honest competitor. It is particularly important that all moneys receive
or expended for campaign purposes should be publicly accounted for
not only after election, but before election as well. Political action mus
be made simpler, easier, and freer from confusion for every citizen.
believe that the prompt removal of unfaithful or incompetent publi
servants should be made easy and sure in whatever way experience shal
show to be most expedient in any given class of cases.

One of the fundamental necessities in a representative governmen
such as ours is to make certain that the men to whom the people dele
gate their power shall serve the people by whom they are elected, an
not the special interests. I believe that every national officer, elected o
appointed, should be forbidden to perform any service or receive any
compensation, directly or indirectly, from interstate corporations; and a
similar provision could not fail to be useful within the states. . . .

All who are acquainted with the effort to remedy industrial abuse
know the type of mind (it may be perfectly honest but is absolutely
fossilized) which declines to allow us to work for the betterment of con
ditions among the wage earners on the ground that we must not inter
fere with the "liberty" of a girl to work under conditions which jeopardize
life and limb, or the "liberty" of a man to work under conditions which
ruin his health after a limited number of years.

Such was the decision. The court was, of course, absolutely powerless to make the remotest attempt to provide a remedy for the wrong which undoubtedly existed, and its refusal to permit action by the state did not confer any power upon the nation to act. The decision was nominally against state's rights, really against popular rights.

Such decisions, arbitrarily and irresponsibly limiting the power of the people, are, of course, fundamentally hostile to every species of real popular government. Representatives of the People of Colorado, here assembled in your legislative capacity, we as a nation should see to it that the people, through their several legislatures, national and state, have complete power of control in all matters that affect the public interest. There should be no means by which any man or set of men could escape the exercise of that control.

We should get the power; that is the first requisite. Now, then, the second is to see that the power be exercised with justice and moderation. The worst enemy of wise conservatism that I know is the type of conservative who tries to prevent wrongs from being remedied because the wrongs have existed for a long time; and, on the other hand, the worst enemy of true progress is the demagogue, or the visionary, who, in the name of progress, leads the people to make blunders such that in the resulting reaction they tend to distrust all progress. Distrust the demagogue and the mere visionary just as you distrust that hide-bound conservative who too often, though an honest man himself, proves to be one of the most efficient friends of corruption. Remember that if you fall into the Scylla of demagogism, on the one hand, it will not help you that you have avoided the Charybdis of corruption and conservatism on the other. If you are in one gulf, it is perfectly true that you are not in the other. But you are in one.

The Progressive Party
Platform of 1912

August 5, 1912

The Progressive party's 1912 platform provides the most ample and ambitious statement of the national legislative aims of Progressivism. It was particularly noteworthy for spelling out in detail a program of social legislation. Although Theodore Roosevelt (Doc. 24) had succeeded in taking the leadership of the party away from La Follette, the platform reflects on most counts the inspiration of La Follette and his admirers. The most controversial plank in the platform, both inside and outside the party, was that on business, since a stronger antitrust statement had been rejected by Roosevelt and his associates. Roosevelt had never abandoned his conviction that an elaborate attack on big business along the lines of the Sherman Anti-Trust Act was futile (see Doc. 28). For his views on this subject he was strongly taken to task by Woodrow Wilson in the campaign (Doc. 35). Kirk H. Porter and Donald Bruce Johnson, National Party Platforms, 1840-1956 (Urbana, 1956), pp. 175-82.

The conscience of the people, in a time of grave national problems, has called into being a new party, born of the nation's sense of justice. We of the Progressive party here dedicate ourselves to the fulfillment of the duty laid upon us by our fathers to maintain the government of the people, by the people and for the people whose foundations they laid. . . .

THE OLD PARTIES

Political parties exist to secure responsible government and to execute the will of the people.

From these great tasks both of the old parties have turned aside. Instead of instruments to promote the general welfare, they have become the tools of corrupt interests which use them impartially to serve their selfish purposes. Behind the ostensible government sits enthroned an invisible government owing no allegiance and acknowledging no responsibility to the people.

To destroy this invisible government, to dissolve the unholy alliance between corrupt business and corrupt politics is the first task of the statesmanship of the day.

The deliberate betrayal of its trust by the Republican party, the fatal incapacity of the Democratic party to deal with the new issues of the new time, have compelled the people to forge a new instrument of government through which to give effect to their will in laws and institutions.

Unhampered by tradition, uncorrupted by power, undismayed by the magnitude of the task, the new party offers itself as the instrument of the people to sweep away old abuses, to build a new and nobler commonwealth. . . .

THE RULE OF THE PEOPLE

. . . . In particular, the party declares for direct primaries for the nomination of State and National officers; for nation-wide preferential primaries for candidates for the presidency; for the direct election of United States Senators by the people; and we urge on the States the policy of the short ballot, with responsibility to the people secured by the initiative, referendum and recall. . . .

EQUAL SUFFRAGE

The Progressive party, believing that no people can justly claim to be a true democracy which denies political rights on account of sex, pledges itself to the task of securing equal suffrage to men and women alike.

CORRUPT PRACTICES

We pledge our party to legislation that will compel strict limitation of all campaign contributions and expenditures, and detailed publicity of both before as well as after primaries and elections.

PUBLICITY AND PUBLIC SERVICE

We pledge our party to legislation compelling the registration of lobbyists; publicity of committee hearings except on foreign affairs, and recording of all votes in committee; and forbidding federal appointees from holding office in State or National political organizations, or taking part as officers or delegates in political conventions for the nomination of elective State or National officials.

THE COURTS

The Progressive party demands such restriction of the power of the courts as shall leave to the people the ultimate authority to determine fundamental questions of social welfare and public policy. To secure this end, it pledges itself to provide:

1. That when an Act, passed under the police power of the State, is held unconstitutional under the State Constitution, by the courts, the people, after an ample interval for deliberation, shall have an opportunity to vote on the question whether they desire the Act to become law, notwithstanding such decision.

2. That every decision of the highest appellate court of a State declaring an Act of the Legislature unconstitutional on the ground of its violation of the Federal Constitution shall be subject to the same review by the Supreme Court of the United States as is now accorded to decisions sustaining such legislation.

ADMINISTRATION OF JUSTICE

. . . . We believe that the issuance of injunctions in cases arising out of labor disputes should be prohibited when such injunctions would not apply when no labor disputes existed.

We believe also that a person cited for contempt in labor disputes, except when such contempt was committed in the actual presence of the court or so near thereto as to interfere with the proper administration of justice, should have a right to trial by jury.

SOCIAL AND INDUSTRIAL JUSTICE

The supreme duty of the Nation is the conservation of human resources through an enlightened measure of social and industrial justice. We pledge ourselves to work unceasingly in State and Nation for:

Effective legislation looking to the prevention of industrial accidents, occupational diseases, overwork, involuntary unemployment, and other injurious effects incident to modern industry;

The fixing of minimum safety and health standards for the various occupations, and the exercise of the public authority of State and Nation, including the Federal Control over interstate commerce, and the taxing power, to maintain such standards;

The prohibition of child labor;

Minimum wage standards for working women, to provide a "living wage" in all industrial occupations;

The general prohibition of night work for women and the establishment of an eight-hour day for women and young persons;

One day's rest in seven for all wage workers;

The eight-hour day in continuous twenty-four-hour industries;

The abolition of the convict contract labor system; substituting a system of prison production for governmental consumption only; and the application of prisoners' earnings to the support of their dependent families;

Publicity as to wages, hours and conditions of labor; full reports upon industrial accidents and diseases; and the opening to public inspection of all tallies, weights, measures and check systems on labor products;

Standards of compensation for death by industrial accident and injury and trade disease which will transfer the burden of lost earnings from the families of working people to the industry, and thus to the community;

The protection of home life against the hazards of sickness, irregular employment and old age through the adoption of a system of social insurance adapted to American use;

The development of the creative labor power of America by lifting the last load of illiteracy from American youth and establishing continuation schools for industrial education under public control and encouraging agricultural education and demonstration in rural schools. . . .

We favor the organization of the workers, men and women, as a means of protecting their interests and of promoting their progress. . . .

BUSINESS

We demand that the test of true prosperity shall be the benefits conferred thereby on all the citizens, not confined to individuals or classes. . . .

We therefore demand a strong National regulation of inter-State corporations. The corporation is an essential part of modern business. The concentration of modern business, in some degree, is both inevitable and necessary for national and international business efficiency. But the existing concentration of vast wealth under a corporate system, unguarded and uncontrolled by the Nation, has placed in the hands of a few men enormous, secret, irresponsible power over the daily life of the citizen—a power insufferable in a free government and certain of abuse. . . .

We urge the establishment of a strong Federal administrative commission of high standing, which shall maintain permanent and active supervision over industrial corporations engaged in inter-State commerce, or such of them as are of public importance. . . .

Such a commission must enforce the complete publicity of those corporate transactions which are of public interest; must attack unfair competition, false capitalization and special privilege. . . .

We favor strengthening the Sherman Law by prohibiting agreemen
to divide territory or limit output; refusing to sell to customers wh
buy from business rivals; to sell below cost in certain areas while main
taining higher prices in other places; using the power of transportatio
to aid or injure special business concerns; and other unfair trade prac
tices.

William Allen White on
The Revival of Democracy
1910

*The information White collected on the democratic uprising in
many American states (see Doc. 21) led him to this optimistic esti-
mation of the value of such reforms as initiative, referendum, and
recall. (See also Doc. 27.) William Allen White, The Old Order
Changeth (New York, 1910), pp. 47-61. Reprinted with the permission of William L. White.*

The rise of democracy in the Middle and Southern states, across the
Mississippi Valley, and along the Pacific coast has been marked by another indication that the people know, either consciously or subcon-
sciously, where the dams are in the current of progress toward self-government. For not merely in the West and South, but all over the
country, the people have passed laws compelling candidates and party
committees to file statements of their expenditures and their sources of
income, and many states have enacted laws limiting the amount of
money that candidates or committees may spend in any primary campaign or in a campaign before a general election. These laws are becoming universal. Publicity of expenses is required of candidates and
party committees in Alabama, West Virginia, Wisconsin, Nebraska,
Kansas, Montana, and Washington; and campaign expenses are limited
either as to amount or as to the right of corporations to contribute in
Arizona, California, Colorado, Missouri, Oklahoma, Nebraska, North
Dakota, Minnesota, Indiana, Pennsylvania, New York, Connecticut, Massachusetts, New Hampshire, Florida, Texas, Oregon, and Arkansas.

The movement to divorce the corporation from politics is so general
that a federal law has been enacted limiting campaign contributions.
And for the first time in the history of the United States the people
know now exactly how much it costs to conduct a national campaign and
from what sources the money comes. No more important step toward
government by the people, for the people, has been taken in this Republic since its beginning. It is true that in many states the law is a
form only; but the fact that it is a law indicates a tendency in American thought which eventually will express itself in custom and usage as
it is now expressed in statute. For when the people know where to
strike at an evil, they always hit it. And it is safe to say that the decree

of divorce between business and politics will be made absolute within a few years. Such flagrant liaisons as that which enacted the tariff bill of 1909 will serve to make the relations between high politics and high finance so obvious that prohibition will be easy. Democracy proposes to put capital out of politics, so that the rights of men where they conflict with the rights of property may be impartially defined. . . .

But the secret ballot, the direct primary, and the purged party—which are now fairly well assured in American politics—do not set the metes and bounds of progress toward self-government in this country. They are fundamental reforms, it is true, and they are the steps that are necessary before there may be any real forward movement. For it will be seen that each one of these movements is a leveling process, a tendency to make money, capital, property, wealth, or financial distinction count for nothing save as an indirect influence in the ballot box. Each of these innovations, the secret ballot, the primary, and the reformed party, is a step toward democracy—a step toward the Declaration of Independence and away from the Constitution, which so feared majority rule that the majority was hedged about with checks and balances at every possible point. In the early days of the Republic the people annulled the Constitution by getting a direct vote on the President, and thus obtained the executive branch of the government. Now they are capturing the legislative branch through the primary, which to-day puts over half the United States senators under the direct vote of the people. When one stops to think that in Oregon, Washington, Nevada, Idaho, California, North Dakota, South Dakota, Nebraska, Kansas, Oklahoma, Texas, Louisiana, Arkansas, Missouri, Iowa, Wisconsin, Ohio, Alabama, Mississippi, Florida, Georgia, Tennessee, South Carolina, Virginia, New Jersey, and Kentucky, United States senators at the next election will go directly to the people for nominations, and not to the railroads and the public service corporations of their respective states, in short, not to capital as they did ten years ago, one realizes how revolutionary are the changes that are coming into our system. The democracy that was gathering strength in the days of Hanna is beginning to move in the nation.

Indeed, the growth of fundamental democracy in this country is astonishing. Thirty years ago the secret ballot was regarded as a passing craze by professional politicians. Twenty years ago it was a vital issue in nearly every American state. To-day the secret ballot is universal in American politics. Ten years ago the direct primary was the subject of an academic discussion in the University of Michigan by a young man named La Follette of Wisconsin. Now it is in active operation in over

two-thirds of our American states, and over half of the American people use the direct primary as a weapon of self-government. Five years
ago the recall was a piece of freak legislation in Oregon. To-day more
American citizens are living under laws giving them the power of recall
than were living under the secret ballot when Garfield came to the
White House, and many times more people have the power to recall
certain public officers to-day than had the advantages of the direct primary form of party nominations when Theodore Roosevelt came to
Washington. The referendum is only five years behind the primary.
Prophecy with these facts before one becomes something more than a
rash guess.

The democracy has the executive and the legislative branches of the
state and federal government under its direct control; for in the nomination of a majority of the members of the House and of the Senate the
personification of property is unimportant. By making the party a legal-
ized state institution, by paying for the party primaries with state taxes,
by requiring candidates at primaries to file their expense accounts and
a list of their contributors (as is done in some states), by limiting the
amount to be spent (as is done in certain states), and by guaranteeing
a secret vote and a fair count, the state has broken the power of money
in politics. Capital is not eliminated from politics, but it is hampered
and circumscribed, and is not the dominant force that it was ten years
ago. Then the political machine was financed by capital invested in
public service corporations and was continually trying to avoid the responsibility of its public partnership. Then the political machine quietly
sold special privileges to public service corporations. Now the political
machine is in a fair way to be reduced to mere political scrap iron by
the rise of the people. To-day in states having the primary under the
state control the corporation candidate for any public office is handi-
capped. The men elected to the United States Senate from states having the Northern type of primary generally have been free men, free
from machine and corporation taint. Under the primary system any
clean, quick-witted man in these states can defeat the corporation senatorial candidate at the primary if the people desire to defeat him. . . .

The people are finding a way around the legislative veto of the state
courts. And this they are doing more generally than may be realized by
many people. The voters are taking two methods of circumventing the
legislative veto of the courts: first, by amending their state constitutions,
or making new constitutions; and, second, by direct legislation, or the
modification of it known as the initiative and referendum. State courts
are elective, and therefore are afraid of majorities. They cannot declare

constitutional amendments unconstitutional, and they handle laws adopted by a direct vote of the people with great care. Hence the prevalence of the constitutional amendment in American states, and the growth of the initiative and referendum from Maine to California. . . . And back of the movement for the initiative and referendum and the primary and the secret ballot, waiting silently for its summons to come to the active service of democracy, like Madame Defarge knitting in the wrongs of the people, stands the recall.

So the appearance of the recall, in the cities of a dozen states within a little over a year, should make those statesmen nervous who look forward to the time when the country will go back to the Good Old Days. For this tightening grip of the people upon their state governments, as evidenced in some form in every American state, has been an intelligent, gradual, well-directed growth of popular power. Its direction has been wise; for from the beginning to the present there has been no spasm of public indignation followed by reaction. Whose wisdom directed it? No man's name is connected with it. No party or propaganda has been behind the movement. . . . It is growth—spiritual growth in the hearts of the American people. It is a big moral movement in democracy.

Herbert Croly on
The Techniques of Democracy
1915

*Herbert Croly was among those who, sympathetic with most of the
Progressive goals, still took a critical view of many Progressive means.
He was particularly skeptical of the effort of some Progressives to
restore popular control through political reforms, especially where
these were not intimately linked with a social program. More doubtful about the enduring value of such reforms than William Allen
White (Doc. 26), he might well have felt himself justified by their
later ineffectuality. (See also Doc. 19.)* Herbert Croly, Progressive
Democracy *(New York, 1915), pp. 211-17. Reprinted with the permission of The Macmillan Company.*

Progressivism means a relation between political and social democracy
which is both mutually dependent and mutually supplementary. Thoroughgoing political democracy is unnecessary and meaningless except
for the purpose of realizing the ideal of social justice. The ideal of social
justice is so exacting and so comprehensive that it cannot be progres-
sively attained by any agency, save by the loyal and intelligent devotion
of the popular will. If democracy is aiming at anything less comprehensive and ultimate than the ideal of social righteousness, this limited
task would be capable of more precise definition and might conceivably
be imposed upon society by Law. But if democracy is aiming at the ideal
of social righteousness, the will of the whole people can be the only possible custodian and creator of so momentous and exacting an enterprise.
The people are made whole by virtue of the consecration of their collective efforts to the realization of an ideal of social justice.

The close connection exhibited in the recent history of the progressive
movement between the increase of popular political power and of social
legislation is an evidence of the necessary formative relation between
political and social democracy. Political democracy is impoverished and
sterile as soon as it becomes divorced from a social program. A social
program becomes dangerous to popular liberty, in case it is not author-
ized by the free choice of the popular will. There is nothing to be
gained by emancipating popular political power, and by providing it
with adequate instruments for the realization of its purposes, unless
this emancipated will is consecrated to the establishment of worthy

moral and social purposes. But a social program which is to be carried out by an increased use of legislative and administrative power cannot be allowed to escape popular control. Effective popular control was not considered necessary under the traditional system, because a supposedly do-nothing government was not dangerous. Even so, . . . the supposedly do-nothing government soon began to assume active and positive functions and was balanced by the organization of a free partisan democracy. But a social program demands much more powerful and efficient government instruments than did the old national economic program, and such instruments must be kept in the most intimate possible relation with the popular will.

The Fathers were entirely justified in believing that the devotion of the people to the ideal of social righteousness could not be taken for granted. Their lawful children at the present day are equally justified in protesting against the extent to which political democrats do take some such devotion for granted. One of the great weaknesses of professional democrats in this country has been their tendency to conceive democracy as essentially a matter of popular political machinery. From their point of view the way to assure the preservation of a democratic social system was to enable the people to vote upon the qualifications of the maximum number of public officials and the maximum number of public measures. They did not pretend that the people could not go wrong; but they conceived democracy as an air-ship with an automatic balancing and stabilizing mechanism. The free use of the ballot box was sufficient to render it proof against fools and knaves. This conception of democracy, precisely because it fails to associate democracy with the conscious realization of a social ideal, always assumes a negative emphasis. Its dominant object is not to give positive momentum and direction to popular rule. It seeks, above all, to prevent the people from being betrayed—from being imposed upon by unpopular policies and unrepresentative officials. But to indoctrinate and organize one's life chiefly for the purpose of avoiding betrayal is to invite sterility and disintegration. Any such negative formulation of the democratic purpose is in point of fact derived from the alliance of the old American democracy with a system of Law which had usurped the essential responsibilities of the popular will, and which had communicated to democracy its own underlying atmosphere of suspicion and apprehension.

If the devotion of the popular will to the ideal of social righteousness cannot be taken for granted, neither can we assume that social righteousness can in the long run be attained by any agency, save by the free conscious and loyal devotion to it of the popular will. At different times in the past benevolent governments, both political and ecclesiastical, have imposed social benefits upon subservient people; but such benefits could never go very far. In proportion as the program of social bene- faction has attained scope and integrity, its wholesome realization has become dependent upon a more active and a more general support from popular public opinion. The amount of assistance which a people can wholesomely receive from the government depends upon the amount of public interest and public spirit which the governmental mechanism and policy demand of them. A government does not become undesir- ably paternal merely as a consequence of the scope of its social program. The policy or the impolicy of its fatherly interest in the welfare of its citizens depends less upon the extent of its active solicitude for them than upon the extent to which this active solicitude is the result of a free and real choice of the popular will. The political system of the United States, even when the government was most limited in its ac- tivities, was always extremely paternal, because it was always seeking to guide the American democracy in the path of righteousness by means of the monarchy of the Law and an aristocracy of the robe, but without any effective consultation with public opinion. A political system in which the government was more active and yet more responsive to the popular will might be essentially less paternal than was the American system when its advocates were most loudly and fondly celebrating its repudiation of paternalism. The more conscious, the more comprehen- sive, and the more enlightened the ideal of social righteousness becomes, the more completely must it be sustained by the explicit, reiterated, and loyal expression of the popular will.

Inasmuch as the connection between the ideal of social righteousness and the popular will cannot be taken for granted, it must be created. It is being created by the faith which underlies progressive democracy. Progressive democracy can no more get along without it than an air- ship can dispense with an engine. Its value should be as widely and as persistently inculcated in a democracy as the worship of the Con- stitution formerly was, for it is the foundation not only of the liberty of the American people, but of their ability to convert civil and politi- cal liberty into a socially desirable consummation.

But the verbal affirmation and inculcation of a faith is only the be- ginning. The loyal devotion to an ideal of social righteousness will not as the mere result of its own affirmative power bring into being social righteousness. The ideal must be embodied in a temporary program. The program must be realized by legislative and administrative action. The governmental action must conform to certain conditions which will serve to make of it an honest step towards the ideal of social democracy. It must be a genuine expression of the popular preference, and it must be adapted to the efficient accomplishment of its immediate purpose. If it conforms to these conditions, it will be constructive not merely in the obvious sense but in the sense of being educational. A nation which does not act sincerely and intelligently in the interest of its collective purpose will not learn much from its own experience. Societies will never be socialized out of scripts, speeches, exhortations and creeds, unless their interest has been aroused, their attention concentrated, and their will disciplined by loyal action on behalf of the social ideal. The attempt to redeem by practical action a comprehensive social responsibility derives its peculiar value less from the probability of any emphatic immediate success than from the demands which it makes upon its supporters. Every specific program which is honestly intended to work for social betterment issues a challenge to its advocates for careful preparation, for disinterested self-devotion, and for a candid appraisal of any possible results. The popular will cannot be sincerely expressed in such a program without also being strengthened and enlightened. A social atmosphere will be created of enterprise, of accomplishment, of moral earnestness, and of inexhaustible curiosity, which will help to make the systematic inculcation of the faith really fruitful.

Progressive democracy is bound to keep its immediate and specific social program disengaged from its ideal of social righteousness. The immediate program is only the temporary instrument, which must be continually reformed and readjusted as a result of the experience gained by its experimental application. . . . It is the torch with which the nation gropes its way in the direction of the star. Dogmatic individualism and dogmatic socialism both conceive their specific programs, their immediate itineraries, as an adequate and a safe guide-book for the entire journey. Progressive democracy must abandon the illusion of any such assurance. No matter how firmly the progressive democrat may believe that his torch is radiating within the limits of its power the light of truth, no matter how confidently he may anticipate an acceleration of speed as a consequence of the increased power of the torch, he must still carefully distinguish between his itinerary and his goal. The goal is sacred. The program is fluid. The pilgrims can trust to the torch only in case they constantly alter and improve it, in order to meet the restless and exacting exigencies of the journey.

The Trusts and Big Business

DOCUMENT TWENTY-EIGHT

Theodore Roosevelt on The Great Corporations

December 3, 1901

In his first annual message to Congress, Theodore Roosevelt stated a view of the problem of big business which in its essentials he never ceased to hold. Big business was an inevitable product of modern industrial organization. The way to cope with its abuses was not to try to break it up, which would be retrograde, but to accept its existence, subject it to regulation, and give to its affairs the widest publicity. These views, which were far more significant than T. R.'s occasional activities as a trustbuster (Doc. 29), provoked intense criticism, particularly within the Progressive movement (Doc. 25) and by Woodrow Wilson during the campaign of 1912 (Doc. 35). H. R. Richardson, Messages and Papers of the Presidents, Vol. XVI, pp. 6645-49.

The tremendous and highly complex industrial development which went on with ever accelerated rapidity during the latter half of the nineteenth century brings us face to face, at the beginning of the twentieth, with very serious social problems. The old laws, and the old customs which had almost the binding force of law, were once quite sufficient to regulate the accumulation and distribution of wealth. Since the industrial changes which have so enormously increased the productive power of mankind, they are no longer sufficient.

The growth of cities has gone on beyond comparison faster than the growth of the country, and the upbuilding of the great industrial centers has meant a startling increase, not merely in the aggregate of wealth, but in the number of very large individual, and especially of very large corporate, fortunes. The creation of these great corporate fortunes has not been due to the tariff nor to any other governmental action, but to natural causes in the business world, operating in other countries as they operate in our own.

The process has aroused much antagonism, a great part of which is wholly without warrant. . . . The captains of industry who have driven the railway systems across this continent, who have built up our commerce, who have developed our manufactures, have on the whole done great good to our people. Without them the material development of which we are so justly proud could never have taken place. . . . The slightest study of business conditions will satisfy anyone capable of forming a judgment that the personal equation is the most important factor in a business operation; that the business ability of the man at the head of any business, big or little, is usually the factor which fixes the gulf between striking success and hopeless failure.

An additional reason for caution in dealing with corporations is to be found in the international commercial conditions of today. . . . Business concerns which have the largest means at their disposal and are managed by the ablest men are naturally those which take the lead in the strife for commercial supremacy among the nations of the world. America has only just begun to assume the commanding position in the international business world which we believe will more and more be hers. It is of the utmost importance that this position be not jeoparded, especially at a time when the overflowing abundance of our own natural resources and the skill, business energy, and mechanical aptitude of our people make foreign markets essential. Under such conditions it would be most unwise to cramp or to fetter the youthful strength of our Nation.

Moreover, it cannot too often be pointed out that to strike with ignorant violence at the interests of one set of men almost inevitably endangers the interests of all. The fundamental rule in our national life —the rule which underlies all others—is that, on the whole, and in the long run, we shall go up or down together. . . .

The mechanism of modern business is so delicate that extreme care must be taken not to interfere with it in a spirit of rashness or ignorance. Many of those who have made it their vocation to denounce the great industrial combinations which are popularly, although with technical inaccuracy, known as "trusts," appeal especially to hatred and fear. These are precisely the two emotions, particularly when combined with ignorance, which unfit men for the exercise of cool and steady judgment. In facing new industrial conditions, the whole history of the world shows that legislation will generally be both unwise and ineffective unless undertaken after calm inquiry. . . .

All this is true; and yet it is also true that there are real and grave evils, one of the chief being over-capitalization, because of its many baleful consequences; and a resolute and practical effort must be made to correct these evils.

There is a widespread conviction . . . that the great corporations known as trusts are in certain of their features and tendencies hurtful to the general welfare. This . . . is based upon sincere conviction that combination and concentration should be, not prohibited, but supervised and within reasonable limits controlled; and in my judgment this conviction is right.

It is no limitation upon property rights or freedom of contract to require that when men receive from government the privilege of doing business under corporate form, which frees them from individual responsibility, and enables them to call into their enterprises the capital of the public, they shall do so upon absolutely truthful representations as to the value of the property in which the capital is to be invested. Corporations engaged in interstate commerce should be regulated if they are found to exercise a license working to the public injury. It should be as much the aim of those who seek for social betterment to rid the business world of crimes of cunning as to rid the entire body politic of crimes of violence. Great corporations exist only because they are created and safe-guarded by our institutions; and it is therefore our right and our duty to see that they work in harmony with these institutions.

The first essential in determining how to deal with the great industrial combinations is knowledge of the facts—publicity. In the interest of the public, the Government should have the right to inspect and examine the workings of the great corporations engaged in interstate business. Publicity is the only sure remedy which we can now invoke. What further remedies are needed in the way of governmental regulation, or taxation, can only be determined after publicity has been obtained. . . . The first requisite is knowledge, full and complete. . . .

The large corporations, commonly called trusts, though organized in one State, always do business in many States, often doing very little business in the State where they are incorporated. There is utter lack of uniformity in the State laws about them; and as no State has any exclusive interest in or power over their acts, it has in practice proved impossible to get adequate regulation through State action. Therefore, in the interest of the whole people, the Nation should, without interfering with the power of the States in the matter itself, also assume power of supervision and regulation over all corporations doing an interstate business. This is especially true where the corporation derives a portion of its wealth from the existence of some monopolistic element or tendency in its business. There would be no hardship in such supervision; banks are subject to it, and in their case it is now accepted as a simple matter of course. Indeed, it is now probable that supervision of corporations by the National Government need not go so far as is now the case with the supervision exercised over them by so conservative a State as Massachusetts, in order to produce excellent results.

When the Constitution was adopted . . . no human wisdom could foretell the sweeping changes, alike in industrial and political conditions, which were to take place by the beginning of the twentieth century. At that time it was accepted as a matter of course that the several States were the proper authorities to regulate, so far as it was then necessary, the comparatively insignificant and strictly localized corporate bodies of the day. The conditions are now wholly different and wholly different action is called for. I believe that a law can be framed which will enable the National Government to exercise control along the lines above indicated; profiting by the experience gained through the passage and administration of the Interstate Commerce Act. If, however, the judgment of the Congress is that it lacks the constitutional power to pass such an act, then a constitutional amendment should be submitted to confer this power.

John Marshall Harlan in
The Northern Securities Case
1904

*Although Roosevelt accepted the principle that large corporations
were here to stay (Doc. 28), he recognized public concern over business consolidation as being in itself a major problem, and took steps
to convince the public that the federal government was big enough
to handle oversized corporations when this was necessary. One of
the most highly publicized and objectionable of business consolidations was the Northern Securities Company, a holding company in
which the Northern Pacific and the Great Northern railroads had
been united, following a spectacular financial struggle between interests led by James J. Hill and Edward H. Harriman. In this emphatically written opinion, Justice John Marshall Harlan upheld the
judgment of a lower federal court that the holding company violated
the Sherman Anti-Trust Act. Four justices dissented from the majority decision. Northern Securities Company v. United States, 193
U. S., 197.*

The Government charges that if the combination was held not to be
in violation of the act of Congress, then all efforts of the National Government to preserve to the people the benefits of free competition
among carriers engaged in interstate commerce will be wholly unavail-
ing, and all transcontinental lines, indeed the entire railway system of
the country, may be absorbed, merged and consolidated, thus placing
the public at the absolute mercy of the holding corporation. . . .

In our judgment, the evidence fully sustains the material allegations
of the bill. . . .

From the decisions in the above cases certain propositions are plainly
deducible and embrace the present case. Those propositions are:

That although the act of Congress known as the Anti-Trust Act has
no reference to the mere manufacture or production of articles or commodities within the limits of the several States, it does embrace and
declare to be illegal every contract, combination or conspiracy, in whatever form, or whatever nature, and whoever may be parties to it, which
directly or necessarily operates *in restraint* of trade or commerce *among
the several States or with foreign nations;*

That the act is not limited to restraints of interstate and international trade or commerce that are unreasonable in their nature, but embraces *all* direct *restraints* imposed by any combination, conspiracy or monopoly upon such trade or commerce;

That railroad carriers engaged in interstate or international commerce are embraced by the act;

That combinations even among *private* manufacturers or dealers whereby *interstate or international commerce* is restrained are equally embraced by the act;

That Congress has the power to establish *rules* by which *interstate and international* commerce shall be governed, and, by the Anti-Trust Act, has prescribed the rule of free competition among those engaged in such commerce;

That *every* combination or conspiracy which would extinguish competition between otherwise competing railroads engaged in *interstate trade or commerce,* and which would *in that way* restrain *such* trade or commerce, is made illegal by the act;

That the natural effect of competition is to increase commerce, and an agreement whose direct effect is to prevent this play of competition restrains instead of promotes trade and commerce;

That to vitiate a combination, such as the act of Congress condemns, it need not be shown that the combination, in fact, results or will result in a total suppression of trade or in a complete monopoly, but it is only essential to show that by its necessary operation it tends to restrain interstate or international trade or commerce and to deprive the public of the advantages that flow from free competition;

That the constitutional guarantee of liberty of contract does not prevent Congress from prescribing the rule of free competition for those engaged in *interstate and international* commerce; and

That under its power to regulate commerce among the several States and with foreign nations, Congress had authority to enact the statute in question. . . .

What the Government particularly complains of, indeed all that it complains of here, is the existence of a combination among the stockholders of competing railroad companies which in violation of the act of Congress restrains interstate and international commerce through the agency of a common corporate trustee designed to act for both companies in repressing free competition between them. . . .

Whether the free operation of the normal law of competition is a wise and wholesome rule for trade and commerce is an economic question which this court need not consider or determine. Undoubtedly, there are those who think that the general business interests and pros-

erity of the country will be best promoted if the rule of competition is
ot applied. But there are others who believe that such a rule is more
ecessary in these days of enormous wealth than it ever was in any
ormer period of our history. Be all this as it may, Congress has, in ef-
ect, recognized the rule of free competition by declaring illegal every
ombination or conspiracy in restraint of interstate and international
ommerce. . . .

Indeed, if the contentions of the defendants are sound, why may not
ll the railway companies in the United States . . . enter into a combi-
ation such as the one here in question, and by the device of a holding
orporation obtain the absolute control throughout the entire country
f rates for passengers and freight, beyond the power of Congress to
rotect the public against their exactions? The argument in behalf of
he defendants necessarily leads to such results and places Congress . . .
1 a condition of utter helplessness, so far as the protection of the public
gainst such combinations is concerned. . . .

Guided by these long-established rules of construction, it is manifest
hat if the Anti-Trust Act is held not to embrace a case such as is now
efore us, the plain intention of the legislative branch of the Govern-
1ent will be defeated. If Congress has not, by the words used in the
ct, described this and like cases, it would, we apprehend, be impossible
› find words that would describe them. . . .

The judgment of the court is that the decree below be and hereby is
ffirmed.

Robert M. La Follette Pleads
For Railroad Regulation

April 23, 1906

This passage is taken from the end of a long and impressive speech delivered in the Senate by La Follette when the Hepburn Act was under debate. La Follette feared that the reform did not go far enough, and was particularly concerned to have the regulation of railroad rates based upon an assessment of the value of their properties and not upon their watered capital. This proposal, rejected in 1906, was embodied in the Progressive party platform (Doc. 25) and incorporated in the Physical Evaluation Act of 1913. The speech was the first La Follette made in the Senate after entering that body. Concerning it his wife wrote to their daughter, Fola: "Whatever comes, he has established himself right in the beginning, as the peer of any man on the floor of the Senate, and a new kind of leader." Fifty-ninth Congress, First Session, Congressional Record, *pp. 5722-23.*

This session of Congress will be but the preliminary skirmish of the great contest to follow. On the day that it is known that only the smallest possible measure of relief has been granted, the movement will begin anew all over the country for a larger concession to public right. That movement *will not* stop until it is completely successful. The only basis upon which it can be settled finally in a free country is a control of the public-service corporations *broad enough, strong enough, and strict enough* to insure justice and equality to all American citizens.

Why pursue a shortsighted, temporizing course? Is it not worse than folly to believe that a country like ours, with all its glorious traditions, will surrender in this war for industrial independence?

Mr. President, the people of this generation have witnessed a revolution which has changed the industrial and commercial life of a nation. They have seen the business system of a century battered down, in violation of State and Federal statutes, and another builded on its ruins.

They know exactly what has happened and why it has happened.

The farmer knows that there is no open, free competitive market for anything he may produce upon his farm. He knows that he must accept the prices arbitrarily fixed by the beef trust and the elevator combine

148

ion. He knows that both of these organizations have been given conrol of the markets by the railroads.

The independent manufacturer knows that he no longer has an open ield and a fairly competitive chance to market his product against the rust with its railroad interests.

The consumer knows that his prices are made for him by those who ontrol the avenues of trade and the highways of commerce. The public as suffered much. It demands relief.

Mr. President, Senators in this discussion have avowed that they were not to be influenced by popular clamor; that they have no sympathy vith bigotry that is blind to great railway enterprise and the value of he services which these corporations render to the public. It has been lenounced as meddlesome interference for anyone to question the right f the railways to fix the markets of this country and to control the lestination of its commerce. Public discussion in support of this legislaion is rebuked as "noisy declamation," and we are advised that public pinion should be scorned; that it is as shifting as the sands of the ea. . . .

Sir, I respect public opinion. I do not fear it. I do not hold it in conempt. The public judgment of this great country forms slowly. It is inelligent. No body of men in this country is superior to it. In a representative democracy the common judgment of the majority must find exression in the law of the land. To deny this is to repudiate the princiles upon which representative democracy is founded.

It is not prejudice nor clamor which is pressing this subject upon the ttention of this body. It is a calm, well-considered public judgment. It s born of conviction—not passion—and it were wise for us to give it eed.

The public has reasoned out its case. For more than a generation of ime it has wrought upon this great question with heart and brain in its aily contact with the great railway corporations. It has mastered all he facts. It is just. It is honest. It is rational. It respects property rights. t well knows that its own industrial and commercial prosperity would ffer and decline if the railroads were wronged, their capital impaired, heir profits unjustly diminished.

But the public refuses longer to recognize this subject as one which he railroads alone have the right to pass upon. It declines longer to pproach it with awe. It no longer regards the railroad schedule as a nystery. It understands the meaning of rebates and "concessions," the vasions through "purchasing agents" and false weights, the subterfuge of "damage claims," the significance of "switching charges," "midnight tariffs," "milling in transit," "tap-line allowances," "underbilling," and "demurrage charges." It comprehends the device known as the "industrial railway," the "terminal railway," and all the tricks of inside companies, each levying tribute upon the traffic. It is quite familiar with the favoritism given to express companies, and knows exactly how producer and consumer have been handed over by the railroads, to be plundered by private car and refrigerator lines, in exchange for their traffic.

The public has gone even deeper into the subject. It knows that transportation is vital to organized society; that it is a function of government; that railway lines are the public highways to market; that these highways are established under the sanction of government; that the railway corporation dictates the location of its right of way, lays its tracks over the property of the citizen without his consent, and that he must market the products of his capital and his labor over this highway, if at all, on the terms fixed by the railway corporation. Or, to say it arrogantly and brutally, as did the president of the Louisville and Nashville Railway Company in his testimony before the Interstate Commerce Commission, that the public can pay the charge which the railroad demands, "or it can walk." In short, sir, the public has come to understand that the railway corporation is a natural monopoly, which has been created by act of government, and that under existing conditions the public is completely at the mercy of this natural monopoly.

Because it is a natural monopoly, because it is the creature of government, it becomes the duty of government to see to it that the railway company inflicts no wrong upon the public, to compel it to do what is right, and to perform its office as a common carrier.

Sir, it is much easier to stand with these great interests than against them. . . .

At no time in the history of any nation has it been so difficult to withstand these forces as it is right here in America to-day. Their power is acknowledged in every community and manifest in every lawmaking body. It is idle to ignore it. There exists all over this country a distrust of Congress, a fear that monopolistic wealth holds the balance of power in legislation.

Mr. President, I contend here, as I have contended upon the public platform in Wisconsin, and in other States, that the history of the last thirty years of struggle for just and equitable legislation demonstrate that the powerful combinations of organized wealth and special interest have had an overbalancing control in State and national legislation.

For a generation the American people have watched the growth of his power in legislation. They observe how vast and far-reaching these modern business methods are in fact. Against the natural laws of trade and commerce is set the arbitrary will of a few masters of special privilege. The principal transportation lines of the country are so operated as to eliminate competition. Between railroads and other monopolies controlling great natural resources and most of the necessaries of life there exists a "community of interests" in all cases and an identity of ownership in many. They have observed that these great combinations are closely associated in business for business reasons; that they are also closely associated in politics for business reasons; that together they constitute a complete system; that they encroach upon the public rights, defeat legislation for the public good, and secure laws to promote private interests.

Is it to be marveled at that the American people have become convinced that railroads and industrial trusts stand between them and their representatives; that they have come to believe that the daily conviction of public officials for betrayal of public trust in municipal, State, and national government is but a suggestion of the potential influence of these great combinations of wealth and power?

During this debate there has been much talk about the country having "hysteria." Magazine writers and press correspondents have been denounced, and there would seem to be an agreement that they are to be pursued and discredited, lest they lodge in the popular mind a wrongful estimate of the public service.

Sir, it does not lie in the power of any or all of the magazines of the country or of the press, great as it is, to destroy, without justification, the confidence of the people in the American Congress. Neither can any man on earth, whatever his position or power, alter the settled conviction of the intelligent citizenship of this country when it is grounded on fact and experience. It rests solely with the United States Senate to fix and maintain its own reputation for fidelity to public trust. It will be judged by the record. It cannot repose in security upon its exalted position and the glorious heritage of its traditions. It is worse than folly to feel, or to profess to feel, indifferent with respect to public judgment. If public confidence is wanting in Congress, it is not of hasty growth, it is not the product of "jaundiced journalism." It is the result of years of disappointment and defeat. It is the outgrowth of a quarter of a century of keen, discriminating study of public questions, public records, and the lives of public men. . . .

For the first time in many years a great measure is before this body for its final action. The subject with which it deals goes to the very heart of the whole question. Out of railroad combination with monopoly and its power over legislation comes the perilous relation which Mr. Justice Brewer says "lifts the corporation into a position of constant danger and menace to republican institutions." . . .

Sir, we have the opportunity to meet the demands of the hour, or we may weakly temporize while the storm continues to gather. . . .

Mr. President, our responsibility is great; our duty is plain. If a true spirit of independent, patriotic service controls Congress, this bill will be reconstructed on the broad basis of public interest.

Woodrow Wilson Calls
For Tariff Revision

April 8, 1913

Wilson appeared in person before a special session of Congress to present an appeal for what he and many Progressives considered to be the long overdue downward revision of the tariff. Since no President after John Adams had appeared before the legislature, Wilson began by telling Congress that he wanted to verify that "the President of the United States is a person, not a mere department of the Government hailing Congress from some isolated island of jealous power." He then launched into this statement on the tariff issue. (For the outcome, see Doc. 32.) H. R. Richardson, Messages and Papers of the Presidents, *Vol. XVI, pp. 7871-73.*

I have called the Congress together in extraordinary session because a duty was laid upon the party now in power at the recent elections which it ought to perform promptly, in order that the burden carried by the people under existing law may be lightened as soon as possible, and in order, also, that the business interests of the country may not be kept too long in suspense as to what the fiscal changes are to be to which they will be required to adjust themselves. It is clear to the whole country that the tariff duties must be altered. They must be changed to meet the radical alteration in the conditions of our economic life which the country has witnessed within the last generation. While the whole face and method of our industrial and commercial life were being changed beyond recognition the tariff schedules have remained what they were before the change began or have moved in the direction they were given when no large circumstance of our industrial development was what it is to-day. Our task is to square them with the actual facts. The sooner that is done the sooner we shall escape from suffering from the facts and the sooner our men of business will be free to thrive by the law of nature (the nature of free business) instead of by the law of legislation and artificial arrangement.

We have seen tariff legislation wander very far afield in our day— very far indeed from the field in which our prosperity might have had a normal growth and stimulation. No one who looks the facts squarely in the face or knows anything that lies beneath the surface of action can fail to perceive the principles upon which recent tariff legislation has been based. We long ago passed beyond the modest notion of "pro-tecting" the industries of the country and moved boldly forward to the idea that they were entitled to the direct patronage of the Government. For a long time—a time so long that the men now active in public policy hardly remember the conditions that preceded it—we have sought in our tariff schedules to give each group of manufacturers or producers what they themselves thought that they needed in order to maintain a practically exclusive market as against the rest of the world. Consciously or unconsciously, we have built up a set of privileges and exemptions from competition behind which it was easy by any, even the crudest, forms of combination to organize monopoly; until at last nothing is normal, nothing is obliged to stand the tests of efficiency and economy, in our world of big business, but everything thrives by concerted arrangement. Only new principles of action will save us from a final hard crystallization of monopoly and a complete loss of the in-fluences that quicken enterprise and keep independent energy alive.

It is plain what those principles must be. We must abolish everything that bears even the semblance of privilege or of any kind of artificial advantage, and put our business men and producers under the stimu-lation of a constant necessity to be efficient, economical, and enter-prising, masters of competitive supremacy, better workers and merchants than any in the world. Aside from the duties laid upon articles which we do not, and probably cannot, produce, therefore, and the duties laid upon luxuries and merely for the sake of the revenues they yield, the object of the tariff duties henceforth laid must be effective compe-tition, the whetting of American wits by contest with the wits of the rest of the world.

It would be unwise to move toward this end headlong, with reckless haste, or with strokes that cut at the very roots of what has grown up amongst us by long process and at our own invitation. It does not alter a thing to upset it and break it and deprive it of a chance to change. It destroys it. We must make changes in our fiscal laws, in our fiscal system, whose object is development, a more free and wholesome de-velopment, not revolution or upset or confusion. We must build up trade, especially foreign trade. We need the outlet and the enlarged field of energy more than we ever did before. We must build up indus-try as well, and must adopt freedom in the place of artificial stimulation only so far as it will build, not pull down. In dealing with the tariff the method by which this may be done will be a matter of judgment, exercised item by item. To some not accustomed to the excitements and responsibilities of greater freedom our methods may in some respects

d at some points seem heroic, but remedies may be heroic and yet
remedies. It is our business to make sure that they are genuine
medies. Our object is clear. If our motive is above just challenge and
ly an occasional error of judgment is chargeable against us, we shall
fortunate.

We are called upon to render the country a great service in more
atters than one. Our responsibility should be met and our methods
ould be thorough, as thorough as moderate and well considered, based
on the facts as they are, and not worked out as if we were beginners.
e are to deal with the facts of our own day, with the facts of no
her, and to make laws which square with those facts. It is best, in-
ed it is necessary, to begin with the tariff. . . .

Woodrow Wilson Assails
The Tariff Lobby

May 26, 1913

When the bill that subsequently became the Underwood Tariff was under debate, lobbyists began to swarm in Washington. Senators and representatives were deluged with petitions and appeals resulting from a massive and well-organized campaign by special interests. For a time, it appeared that the same interests which had helped Senator Aldrich (Doc. 22) and other conservatives to cripple reforms at the time of the Payne-Aldrich Tariff of 1909 would succeed again. Wilson then boldly issued this public statement about the tariff lobby. "The country is indebted to President Wilson," said Senator La Follette, "for exploding the bomb that blew the lid off the congressional lobby." La Follette himself started an investigation of the lobbyists, and, under the pressure of such publicity and disclosure, the Underwood Tariff was passed. It brought an average downward adjustment of duties of about eleven per cent. One of its notable features was a modest income tax provision, made possible by the recent ratification of the Sixteenth Amendment. (See also Doc. 31.) Woodrow Wilson, "Statement to the Press," New York Times, May 27, 1913.

I think that the public ought to know the extraordinary exertion being made by the lobby in Washington to gain recognition for certain alterations of the tariff bill. Washington has seldom seen so numerous, so industrious, or so insidious a lobby. The newspapers are being filled with paid advertisements calculated to mislead the judgement of public men not only, but also the public opinion of the country itself. There is every evidence that money without limit is being spent to sustain this lobby, and to create an appearance of a pressure of public opinion antagonistic to some of the chief items of the tariff bill.

It is of serious interest to the country that the people at large should have no lobby and be voiceless in these matters, while great bodies of astute men seek to create an artificial opinion and to overcome the interests of the public for their private profit. It is thoroughly worth the while of the people of this country to take knowledge of this matter. Only public opinion can check and destroy it.

The Government in all its branches ought to be relieved from this intolerable burden and this constant interruption to the calm progress of debate. I know that in this I am speaking for the members of the two houses who would rejoice as much as I would to be released from this unbearable situation.

The Pujo Committee on
The Money Trust

1913

*Representative Arsène Pujo of Louisiana was a member of the Na-
tional Monetary Commission of 1908, established to make recommendations on the reorganization of the American banking system.
He was one of those dissatisfied with Senator Nelson W. Aldrich's
(Doc. 22) domination of the commission and with the conservatism
of its report. Consequently, as Chairman of the House Banking and
Currency Committee, he received authorization from Congress in
1912 to investigate the ramifications of the "money trust." After
extended questioning of bankers and businessmen, the Pujo Committee issued a report on the vote of the investment bankers of
which this excerpt is a small portion. Its findings were popularized
by Louis D. Brandeis in* Other People's Money *(Doc. 34) and may
have had considerable influence on provisions of the Federal Reserve
Act. Sixty-second Congress, Third Session.,* House Report No. 1593,
Vol. III, pp. 55ff.

This increased concentration of control of money and credit has been
effected principally as follows:

First, through consolidations of competitive or potentially competitiv
banks and trust companies, which consolidations in turn have recentl
been brought under sympathetic management.

Second, through the same powerful interests becoming large stock
holders in potentially competitive banks and trust companies. This i
the simplest way of acquiring control, but since it requires the larges
investment of capital, it is the least used, although the recent inves
ments in that direction for that apparent purpose amount to tens c
millions of dollars in present market values.

Third, through the confederation of potentially competitive bank
and trust companies by means of the system of interlocking directorate

Fourth, through the influence which the more powerful bankin
houses, banks, and trust companies have secured in the management c
insurance companies, railroads, producing and trading corporations, an
public utility corporations, by means of stockholdings, voting trust
fiscal agency contracts, or representation upon their boards of director
or through supplying the money requirements of railway, industria

and public utilities corporations and thereby being enabled to participate in the determination of their financial and business policies.

Fifth, through partnership or joint account arrangements between a
few of the leading banking houses, banks, and trust companies in the
purchase of security issues of the great interstate corporations, accompanied by understandings of recent growth—sometimes called "banking
ethics"—which have had the effect of effectually destroying competition
between such banking houses, banks, and trust companies in the struggle
for business or in the purchase and sale of large issues of such securities.

SECTION 4—AGENTS OF CONCENTRATION

It is a fair deduction from the testimony that the most active agents
in forwarding and bringing about the concentration of control of money
and credit through one or another of the processes above described
have been and are—

J. P. Morgan & Co.
First National Bank of New York
National City Bank of New York
Lee, Higginson & Co., of Boston and New York
Kidder, Peabody & Co., of Boston and New York
Kuhn, Loeb & Co. . . .

Summary of Directorships Held by These Members of the Group . . .
shows the combined directorship in the more important enterprises
held by Morgan & Co., the First National Bank, the National City Bank,
and the Bankers and Guaranty Trust Cos., which latter two, as previously shown, are absolutely controlled by Morgan & Co. through voting
trusts. It appears there that firm members or directors of these institutions together hold:

One hundred and eighteen directorships in 34 banks and trust companies having total resources of $2,679,000,000 and total deposits of
$1,983,000,000.

Thirty directorships in 10 insurance companies having total assets of
$2,293,000,000.

One hundred and five directorships in 32 transportation systems having a total capitalization of $11,784,000,000 and a total mileage (exclud-
ing express companies and steamship lines) of 150,200.

Sixty-three directorships in 24 producing and trading corporations
having a total capitalization of $3,339,000,000.

Twenty-five directorships in 12 public utility corporations having a total capitalization of $2,150,000,000.

In all, 341 directorships in 112 corporations having aggregate resources or capitalization of $22,245,000,000.

The members of the firm of J. P. Morgan & Co. hold 72 directorships in 47 of the greater corporations; George F. Baker, chairman of the board, F. L. Hine, president, and George F. Baker, Jr., and C. D. Norton, vice-presidents, of the First National Bank of New York, hold 46 directorships in 37 of the greater corporations; and James Stillman, chairman of the board, Frank A. Vanderlip, president, and Samuel McRoberts, J. T. Talbert, W. A. Simonson, vice-presidents, of the National City Bank of New York, hold 32 directorships in 26 of the greater corporations; making in all for these members of the group 150 directorships in 110 of the greater corporations.

Louis D. Brandeis on
The Uses of Other People's Money
1914

As soon as the report of the Pujo Committee (Doc. 33) was pub-
lished, Louis D. Brandeis wired its counsel for a copy, and, having
read it, reported: "It is admirable, and most of your recommenda-
tions I should heartily approve. In some respects it seems to me that
the recommendations do not go far enough." Believing that "no
economic problem in America is as important today as that presented
by the Money Trust—the control which a few financiers exercise
over the capital of America," he set about to explore the implications
of the committee's findings in a series of articles in Harper's
Weekly, *later published in book form by Frederick A. Stokes Co.*
Louis D. Brandeis, Other People's Money, *pp. 4-19.*

The dominant element in our financial oligarchy is the investment
banker. Associated banks, trust companies and life insurance companies
are his tools. Controlled railroads, public service and industrial corporations are his subjects. Though properly but middlemen, these bankers
bestride as masters America's business world, so that practically no large
enterprise can be undertaken successfully without their participation or
approval. These bankers are, of course, able men possessed of large fortunes; but the most potent factor in their control of business is not the
possession of extraordinary ability or huge wealth. The key to their
power is Combination—concentration intensive and comprehensive—
advancing on three distinct lines:

First: There is the obvious consolidation of banks and trust companies;
the less obvious affiliations—through stockholdings, voting trusts and
interlocking directorates—of banking institutions which are not legally
connected; and the joint transactions, gentlemen's agreements and "banking ethics" which eliminate competition among the investment bankers.

Second: There is the consolidation of railroads into huge systems, the
large combinations of public service corporations and the formation of
industrial trusts, which, by making businesses so "big" that local, independent banking concerns cannot alone supply the necessary funds, has
created dependence upon the associated New York bankers.

But combination, however intensive, along these lines only, could not have produced the Money Trust—another and more potent factor of combination was added.

Third: Investment bankers, like J. P. Morgan & Co., dealers in bonds, stocks and notes, encroached upon the functions of the three other classes of corporations with which their business brought them into contact. They became the directing power in railroads, public service and industrial companies through which our great business operations are conducted—the makers of bonds and stocks. They became the directing power in the life insurance companies, and other corporate reservoirs of the people's savings—the buyers of bonds and stocks. They became the directing power also in banks and trust companies—the depositaries of the quick capital of the country—the life blood of business, with which they and others carried on their operations. Thus four distinct functions, each essential to business, and each exercised, originally, by a distinct set of men, became united in the investment banker. It is to this union of business functions that the existence of the Money Trust is mainly due.*

The development of our financial oligarchy followed, in this respect, lines with which the history of political despotism has familiarized us— usurpation, proceeding by gradual encroachment rather than by violent acts; subtle and often long-concealed concentration of distinct functions, which are beneficent when separately administered, and dangerous only when combined in the same persons. It was by processes such as these that Cæsar Augustus became master of Rome. The makers of our own Constitution had in mind like dangers to our political liberty when they provided so carefully for the separation of governmental powers.

THE PROPER SPHERE OF THE INVESTMENT BANKER

The original function of the investment banker was that of dealer in bonds, stocks and notes; buying mainly at wholesale from corporations, municipalities, states and governments which need money, and selling to those seeking investments. The banker performs, in this respect, the function of a merchant; and the function is a very useful one. Large business enterprises are conducted generally by corporations. The permanent capital of corporations is represented by bonds and stocks. The bonds and stocks of the more important corporations are owned, in large part, by small investors, who do not participate in the management of the company. Corporations require the aid of a banker-middleman,

---

* Obviously only a few of the investment bankers exercise this great power; but many others perform important functions in the system, as hereinafter described.

for they lack generally the reputation and clientele essential to selling their own bonds and stocks direct to the investor. Investors in corporate securities, also, require the services of a banker-middleman. The number of securities upon the market is very large. Only a part of these securities is listed on the New York Stock Exchange; but its listings alone comprise about sixteen hundred different issues aggregating about $26,500,000,000, and each year new listings are made averaging about two hundred and thirty-three to an amount of $1,500,000,000. For a small investor to make an intelligent selection from these many corporate securities—indeed, to pass an intelligent judgment upon a single one—is ordinarily impossible. He lacks the ability, the facilities, the training and the time essential to a proper investigation. Unless his purchase is to be little better than a gamble, he needs the advice of an expert, who, combining special knowledge with judgment, has the facilities and incentive to make a thorough investigation. This dependence, both of corporations and of investors, upon the banker has grown in recent years, since women and others who do not participate in the management have become the owners of so large a part of the stocks and bonds of our great corporations. Over half of the stockholders of the American Sugar Refining Company and nearly half of the stockholders of the Pennsylvania Railroad and of the New York, New Haven & Hartford Railroad are women.

Good-will—the possession by a dealer of numerous and valuable regular customers—is always an important element in merchandising. But in the business of selling bonds and stocks, it is of exceptional value, for the very reason that the small investor relies so largely upon the banker's judgment. This confidential relation of the banker to customers—and the knowledge of the customers' private affairs acquired incidentally— is often a determining factor in the marketing of securities. With the advent of Big Business such good-will possessed by the older banking houses, preëminently J. P. Morgan & Co. and their Philadelphia House called Drexel & Co., by Lee, Higginson & Co. and Kidder, Peabody & Co. of Boston, and by Kuhn, Loeb & Co. of New York, became of enhanced importance. The volume of new security issues was greatly increased by huge railroad consolidations, the development of the holding companies and particularly by the formation of industrial trusts. The rapidly accumulating savings of our people sought investment. The field of operations for the dealer in securities was thus much enlarged. And, as the securities were new and untried, the services of the investment banker were in great demand, and his powers and profits increased accordingly.

CONTROLLING THE SECURITY-MAKERS

But this enlargement of their legitimate field of operations did not satisfy investment bankers. They were not content merely to deal in securities. They desired to manufacture them also. They became promoters, or allied themselves with promoters. Thus it was that J. P. Morgan & Company formed the Steel Trust, the Harvester Trust and the Shipping Trust. And, adding the duties of undertaker to those of midwife, the investment bankers became, in times of corporate disaster members of security-holders' "Protective Committees"; then they participated as "Reorganization Managers" in the reincarnation of the unsuccessful corporations and ultimately became directors. It was in this way that the Morgan associates acquired their hold upon the Southern Railway, the Northern Pacific, the Reading, the Erie, the Père Marquette, the Chicago and Great Western, and the Cincinnati, Hamilton & Dayton. Often they insured the continuance of such control by the device of the voting trust; but even where no voting trust was created, a secure hold was acquired upon reorganization. It was in this way also that Kuhn, Loeb & Co. became potent in the Union Pacific and in the Baltimore & Ohio.

But the banker's participation in the management of corporations was not limited to cases of promotion or reorganization. An urgent or extensive need of new money was considered a sufficient reason for the banker's entering a board of directors. Often without even such excuse the investment banker has secured a place upon the Board of Directors, through his powerful influence or the control of his customers' proxies. Such seems to have been the fatal entrance of Mr. Morgan into the management of the then prosperous New York, New Haven & Hartford Railroad, in 1892. When once a banker has entered the Board—whatever may have been the occasion—his grip proves tenacious and his influence usually supreme; for he controls the supply of new money.

The investment banker is naturally on the lookout for good bargains in bonds and stocks. Like other merchants, he wants to buy his merchandise cheap. But when he becomes director of a corporation, he occupies a position which prevents the transaction by which he acquires its corporate securities from being properly called a bargain. Can there be real bargaining when the same man is on both sides of a trade? The investment banker, through his controlling influence on the Board of Directors, decides that the corporation shall issue and sell the securities, decides the price at which it shall sell them, and decides that it shall sell the securities to himself. The fact that there are other directors besides the banker on the Board does not, in practice, prevent this being the result. The banker, who holds the purse-strings, becomes usually the dominant spirit. Through voting-trusteeships, exclusive financial agencies, membership on executive or finance committees, or by mere directorships, J. P. Morgan & Co., and their associates, held such financial power in at least thirty-two transportation systems, public utility corporations and industrial companies—companies with an aggregate capitalization of $17,273,000,000. Mainly for corporations so controlled, J. P. Morgan & Co. procured the public marketing in ten years of security issues aggregating $1,950,000,000. This huge sum does not include any issues marketed privately, nor any issues, however marketed, of intra-state corporations. Kuhn, Loeb & Co. and a few other investment bankers exercise similar control over many other corporations.

CONTROLLING SECURITY-BUYERS

Such control of railroads, public service and industrial corporations assures to the investment bankers an ample supply of securities at attractive prices; and merchandise well bought is half sold. But these bond and stock merchants are not disposed to take even a slight risk as to their ability to market their goods. They saw that if they could control the security-buyers, as well as the security-makers, investment banking would, indeed, be "a happy hunting ground"; and they have made it so.

The numerous small investors cannot, in the strict sense, be controlled; but their dependence upon the banker insures their being duly influenced. A large part, however, of all bonds issued and of many stocks are bought by the prominent corporate investors; and most prominent among these are the life insurance companies, the trust companies, and the banks. The purchase of a security by these institutions not only relieves the banker of the merchandise, but recommends it strongly to the small investor, who believes that these institutions are wisely managed. These controlled corporate investors are not only large customers, but may be particularly accommodating ones. Individual investors are moody. They buy only when they want to do so. They are sometimes inconveniently reluctant. Corporate investors, if controlled, may be made to buy when the bankers need a market. It was natural that the investment bankers proceeded to get control of the great life insurance companies, as well as of the trust companies and the banks.

The field thus occupied is uncommonly rich. The life insurance companies are our leading institutions for savings. Their huge surplus and reserves, augmented daily, are always clamoring for investment. No panic or money shortage stops the inflow of new money from the perennial stream of premiums on existing policies and interest on existing investments. The three great companies—the New York Life, the Mutual of New York, and the Equitable—would have over $55,000,000 of *new* money to invest annually, even if they did not issue a single new policy. In 1904—just before the Armstrong investigation—these three companies had together $1,247,331,738.18 of assets. They had issued in that year $1,025,671,126 of new policies. The New York legislature placed in 1906 certain restrictions upon their growth; so that their new business since has averaged $547,384,212, or only fifty-three per cent of what it was in 1904. But the aggregate assets of these companies increased in the last eight years to $1,817,052,260.36. At the time of the Armstrong investigation the average age of these three companies was fifty-six years. *The growth of assets in the last eight years was about half as large as the total growth in the preceding fifty-six years.* These three companies must invest annually about $70,000,000 of new money; and besides, many old investments expire or are changed and the proceeds must be reinvested. A large part of all life insurance surplus and reserves are invested in bonds. The aggregate bond investments of these three companies on January 1, 1913, was $1,019,153,268.93.

It was natural that the investment bankers should seek to control these never-failing reservoirs of capital. George W. Perkins was Vice-President of the New York Life, the largest of the companies. While remaining such he was made a partner in J. P. Morgan & Co., and in the four years preceding the Armstrong investigation, his firm sold the New York Life $38,804,918.51 in securities. The New York Life is a mutual company, supposed to be controlled by its policy-holders. But, as the Pujo Committee finds, "the so-called control of life insurance companies by policy-holders through mutualization is a farce" and "its only result is to keep in office a self-constituted, self-perpetuating management."

The Equitable Life Assurance Society is a stock company and is controlled by $100,000 of stock. The dividend on this stock is limited by law to seven per cent; but in 1910 Mr. Morgan paid about $3,000,000 for $51,000 par value of this stock, or $5,882.35 a share. The dividend return on the stock investment is less than one-eighth of one per cent; but the assets controlled amount now to over $500,000,000. And certain of these assets had an especial value for investment bankers—namely, the large holdings of stock in banks and trust companies.

The Armstrong investigation disclosed the extent of financial power exerted through the insurance company holdings of bank and trust company stock. The Committee recommended legislation compelling the insurance companies to dispose of the stock within five years. A law to that effect was enacted, but the time was later extended. The companies then disposed of a part of their bank and trust company stocks; but, as the insurance companies were controlled by the investment bankers, these gentlemen sold the bank and trust company stocks to themselves.

Referring to such purchases from the Mutual Life, as well as from the Equitable, the Pujo Committee found:

> Here, then, were stocks of five important trust companies and one of our largest national banks in New York City that had been held by these two life insurance companies. Within five years all of these stocks, so far as distributed by the insurance companies, have found their way into the hands of the men who virtually controlled or were identified with the management of the insurance companies or of their close allies and associates, to that extent thus further entrenching them.

The banks and trust companies are depositaries, in the main, not of the people's savings, but of the business man's quick capital. Yet, since the investment banker acquired control of banks and trust companies, these institutions also have become, like the life companies, large purchasers of bonds and stocks. Many of our national banks have invested in this manner a large part of all their resources, including capital, surplus and deposits. The bond investments of some banks exceed by far the aggregate of their capital and surplus, and nearly equal their loanable deposits.

CONTROLLING OTHER PEOPLE'S QUICK CAPITAL

The goose that lays golden eggs has been considered a most valuable possession. But even more profitable is the privilege of taking the golden eggs laid by somebody else's goose. The investment bankers and their associates now enjoy that privilege. They control the people through the people's own money. If the bankers' power were commensurate only with their wealth, they would have relatively little influence on American business. Vast fortunes like those of the Astors are no doubt regrettable. They are inconsistent with democracy. They are unsocial. And they seem peculiarly unjust when they represent largely unearned increment. But the wealth of the Astors does not endanger political or industrial liberty. It is insignificant in amount as compared with the aggregate wealth of America, or even of New York City. It lacks significance largely because its owners have only the income from their own wealth. The Astor wealth is static. The wealth of the Morgan associates is dynamic. The power and the growth of power of our financial oligarchs comes from wielding the savings and quick capital of others. In two of the three great life insurance companies the influence of J. P. Morgan & Co. and their associates is exerted without any individual investment by them whatsoever. Even in the Equitable, where Mr. Morgan bought an actual majority of all the outstanding stock, his investment amounts to little more than one-half of one per cent of the assets of the company. The fetters which bind the people are forged from the people's own gold.

Woodrow Wilson on
The Meaning of the New Freedom
1912

Wilson could not accept the idea, so often expressed by Roosevelt (Doc. 28), that large corporations are inevitable. He believed far more ardently in breaking them up, along the lines promised by the Sherman Act, arguing that any government that tried only to control big business would itself be dominated by the very corporations it sought to govern. He believed that both democracy and free enterprise depended upon an assault on the illicit large businesses, though he had difficulty in explaining how this assault could be safely carried on (See Doc. 36). In his 1912 campaign speeches, gathered later into The New Freedom, *he explained his own conceptions of freedom and enterprise, no doubt voicing at the same time the feelings of a great many Americans engaged in farming and small business. Woodrow Wilson,* The New Freedom *(New York, 1913), pp. 5-7, 13-20, 58-65, 193-96, 200-203, 206-208. Also available in the Spectrum Classics in History Series.*

We have come upon a very different age from any that preceded us. We have come upon an age when we do not do business in the way in which we used to do business—when we do not carry on any of the operations of manufacture, sale, transportation, or communication as men used to carry them on. There is a sense in which in our day the individual has been submerged. In most parts of our country men work, not for themselves, not as partners in the old way in which they used to work, but generally as employees—in a higher or lower grade—of great corporations. There was a time when corporations played a very minor part in our business affairs, but now they play the chief part, and most men are the servants of corporations.

You know what happens when you are the servant of a corporation. You have in no instance access to the men who are really determining the policy of the corporation. If the corporation is doing the things that it ought not to do, you really have no voice in the matter and must obey the orders, and you have oftentimes with deep mortification to co-operate in the doing of things which you know are against the public interest. Your individuality is swallowed up in the individuality and purpose of a great organization.

It is true that, while most men are thus submerged in the corporation, a few, a very few, are exalted to a power which as individuals they could never have wielded. Through the great organizations of which they are the heads, a few are enabled to play a part unprecedented by anything in history in the control of the business operations of the country and in the determination of the happiness of great numbers of people.

Yesterday, and ever since history began, men were related to one another as individuals. To be sure there were the family, the Church, and the State, institutions which associated men in certain wide circles of relationship. But in the ordinary concerns of life, in the ordinary work, in the daily round, men dealt freely and directly with one another. To-day, the everyday relationships of men are largely with great impersonal concerns, with organizations, not with other individual men.

Now this is nothing short of a new social age, a new era of human relationships, a new stage-setting for the drama of life. . . .

Since I entered politics, I have chiefly had men's views confided to me privately. Some of the biggest men in the United States, in the field of commerce and manufacture, are afraid of somebody, are afraid of something. They know that there is a power somewhere so organized, so subtle, so watchful, so interlocked, so complete, so pervasive, that they had better not speak above their breath when they speak in condemnation of it.

They know that America is not a place of which it can be said, as it used to be, that a man may choose his own calling and pursue it just as far as his abilities enable him to pursue it; because to-day, if he enters certain fields, there are organizations which will use means against him that will prevent his building up a business which they do not want to have built up; organizations that will see to it that the ground is cut from under him and the markets shut against him. For if he begins to sell to certain retail dealers, to any retail dealers, the monopoly will refuse to sell to those dealers, and those dealers, afraid, will not buy the new man's wares. . . .

American industry is not free, as once it was free; American enterprise is not free; the man with only a little capital is finding it harder to get into the field, more and more impossible to compete with the big fellow. Why? Because the laws of this country do not prevent the strong from crushing the weak. That is the reason, and because the strong have crushed the weak the strong dominate the industry and the economic life of this country. No man can deny that the lines of endeavor have more and more narrowed and stiffened; no man who knows anything about the development of industry in this country can have failed to observe that the larger kinds of credit are more and more difficult to obtain, unless you obtain them upon the terms of uniting your efforts with those who already control the industries of the country; and nobody can fail to observe that any man who tries to set himself up in competition with any process of manufacture which has been taken under the control of large combinations of capital will presently find himself either squeezed out or obliged to sell and allow himself to be absorbed.

There is a great deal that needs reconstruction in the United States. I should like to take a census of the business men—I mean the rank and file of the business men—as to whether they think that business conditions in this country, or rather whether the organization of business in this country, is satisfactory or not. I know what they would say if they dared. If they could vote secretly they would vote overwhelmingly that the present organization of business was meant for the big fellows and was not meant for the little fellows; that it was meant for those who are at the top and was meant to exclude those who are at the bottom; that it was meant to shut out beginners, to prevent new entries in the race, to prevent the building up of competitive enterprises that would interfere with the monopolies which the great trusts have built up.

What this country needs above everything else is a body of laws which will look after the men who are on the make rather than the men who are already made. Because the men who are already made are not going to live indefinitely, and they are not always kind enough to leave sons as able and honest as they are.

The originative part of America, the part of America that makes new enterprises, the part into which the ambitious and gifted workingman makes his way up, the class that saves, that plans, that organizes, that presently spreads its enterprises until they have a national scope and character—that middle class is being more and more squeezed out by the processes which we have been taught to call processes of prosperity. Its members are sharing prosperity, no doubt; but what alarms me is that they are not *originating* prosperity. No country can afford to have its prosperity originated by a small controlling class. The treasury of America does not lie in the brains of the small body of men now in control of the great enterprises that have been concentrated under the direction of a very small number of persons. The treasury of America lies in those ambitions, those energies, that cannot be restricted to a special favored class. It depends upon the inventions of unknown men, upon the originations of unknown men, upon the ambitions of unknown men.

Every country is renewed out of the ranks of the unknown, not out of the ranks of those already famous and powerful and in control.

There has come over the land that un-American set of conditions which enables a small number of men who control the government to get favors from the government; by those favors to exclude their fellows from equal business opportunity; by those favors to extend a network of control that will presently dominate every industry in the country, and so make men forget the ancient time when America lay in every hamlet, when America was to be seen in every fair valley, when America displayed her great forces on the broad prairies, ran her fine fires of enterprise up over the mountainsides and down into the bowels of the earth, and eager men were everywhere captains of industry, not employees; not looking to a distant city to find out what they might do, but looking about among their neighbors, finding credit according to their character, not according to their connections, finding credit in proportion to what was known to be in them and behind them, not in proportion to the securities they held that were approved where they were not known. In order to start an enterprise now, you have to be authenticated, in a perfectly impersonal way, not according to yourself, but according to what you own that somebody else approves of your owning. You cannot begin such an enterprise as those that have made America until you are so authenticated, until you have succeeded in obtaining the good-will of large allied capitalists. Is that freedom? That is dependence, not freedom.

We used to think in the old-fashioned days when life was very simple that all that government had to do was to put on a policeman's uniform, and say, "Now don't anybody hurt anybody else." We used to say that the ideal of government was for every man to be left alone and not interfered with, except when he interfered with somebody else; and that the best government was the government that did as little governing as possible. That was the idea that obtained in Jefferson's time. But we are coming now to realize that life is so complicated that we are not dealing with the old conditions, and that the law has to step in and create new conditions under which we may live, the conditions which will make it tolerable for us to live. . . .

The government of the United States at present is a foster-child of the special interests. It is not allowed to have a will of its own. It is told at every move: "Don't do that; you will interfere with our prosperity." And when we ask, "Where is our prosperity lodged?" a certain group of gentlemen say, "With us." The government of the United

States in recent years has not been administered by the common people of the United States. You know just as well as I do—it is not an indictment against anybody, it is a mere statement of the facts—that the people have stood outside and looked on at their own government and that all they have had to determine in past years has been which crowd they would look on at; whether they would look on at this little group or that little group who had managed to get the control of affairs in its hands. Have you ever heard, for example, of any hearing before any great committee of the Congress in which the people of the country as a whole were represented, except it may be by the Congressmen themselves? The men who appear at those meetings in order to argue for or against a schedule in the tariff, for this measure or against that measure, are men who represent special interests. They may represent them very honestly, they may intend no wrong to their fellow-citizens, but they are speaking from the point of view always of a small portion of the population. I have sometimes wondered why men, particularly men of means, men who didn't have to work for their living, shouldn't constitute themselves attorneys for the people, and every time a hearing is held before a committee of Congress should not go and ask: "Gentlemen, in considering these things suppose you consider the whole country? Suppose you consider the citizens of the United States?"

I don't want a smug lot of experts to sit down behind closed doors in Washington and play Providence to me. There is a Providence to which I am perfectly willing to submit. But as for other men setting up as Providence over myself, I seriously object. I have never met a political savior in the flesh, and I never expect to meet one. . . .

I am one of those who absolutely reject the trustee theory, the guardianship theory. I have never found a man who knew how to take care of me, and, reasoning from that point out, I conjecture that there isn't any man who knows how to take care of all the people of the United States. I suspect that the people of the United States understand their own interests better than any group of men in the confines of the country understand them. The men who are sweating blood to get their foothold in the world of endeavor understand the conditions of business in the United States very much better than the men who have arrived and are at the top. They know what the thing is that they are struggling against. They know how difficult it is to start a new enterprise. They know how far they have to search for credit that will put them upon an even footing with the men who have already built up industry in this country. They know that somewhere, by somebody, the development of industry is being controlled. . . .

The government of our country cannot be lodged in any special class. The policy of a great nation cannot be tied up with any particular set of interests. I want to say, again and again, that my arguments do not touch the character of the men to whom I am opposed. I believe that the very wealthy men who have got their money by certain kinds of corporate enterprise have closed in their horizon, and that they do not see and do not understand the rank and file of the people. It is for that reason that I want to break up the little coterie that has determined what the government of the nation should do. The list of the men who used to determine what New Jersey should and should not do did not exceed half a dozen, and they were always the same men. These very men now are, some of them, frank enough to admit that New Jersey has finer energy in her because more men are consulted and the whole field of action is widened and liberalized. We have got to relieve our government from the domination of special classes, not because these special classes are bad, necessarily, but because no special class can understand the interests of a great community.

I believe, as I believe in nothing else, in the average integrity and the average intelligence of the American people, and I do not believe that the intelligence of America can be put into commission anywhere. I do not believe that there is any group of men of any kind to whom we can afford to give that kind of trusteeship.

I will not live under trustees if I can help it. No group of men less than the majority has a right to tell me how I have got to live in America. I will submit to the majority, because I have been trained to do it —though I may sometimes have my private opinion even of the majority. I do not care how wise, how patriotic, the trustees may be, I have never heard of any group of men in whose hands I am willing to lodge the liberties of America in trust. . . .

Mr. Roosevelt attached to his platform some very splendid suggestions as to noble enterprises which we ought to undertake for the uplift of the human race; but when I hear an ambitious platform put forth, I am very much more interested in the dynamics of it than in the rhetoric of it. I have a very practical mind, and I want to know who are going to do those things and how they are going to be done. If you have read the trust plank in that platform as often as I have read it, you have found it very long, but very tolerant. It did not anywhere condemn monopoly, except in words; its essential meaning was that the trusts have been bad and must be made to be good. You know that Mr. Roosevelt long ago classified trusts for us as good and bad, and he said that he was afraid only of the bad ones. Now he does not desire that there should be any more bad ones, but proposes that they should all be made good by discipline, directly applied by a commission of executive appointment. All he explicitly complains of is lack of publicity and lack of fairness; not the exercise of power, for throughout that plank the power of the great corporations is accepted as the inevitable consequence of the modern organization of industry. All that it is proposed to do is to take them under control and regulation. The national administration having for sixteen years been virtually under the regulation of the trusts, it would be merely a family matter were the parts reversed and were the other members of the family to exercise the regulation. And the trusts, apparently, which might, in such circumstances, comfortably continue to administer our affairs under the mollifying influences of the federal government, would then, if you please, be the instrumentalities by which all the humanistic, benevolent program of the rest of that interesting platform would be carried out!

I have read and reread that plank, so as to be sure that I get it right. All that it complains of is—and the complaint is a just one, surely—that these gentlemen exercise their power in a way that is secret. Therefore, we must have publicity. Sometimes they are arbitrary; therefore they need regulation. Sometimes they do not consult the general interests of the community; therefore they need to be reminded of those general interests by an industrial commission. But at every turn it is the trusts who are to do us good, and not we ourselves.

Again, I absolutely protest against being put into the hands of trustees. Mr. Roosevelt's conception of government is Mr. Taft's conception, that the Presidency of the United States is the presidency of a board of directors. I am willing to admit that if the people of the United States cannot get justice for themselves, then it is high time that they should join the third party and get it from somebody else. The justice proposed is very beautiful; it is very attractive; there were planks in that platform which stir all the sympathies of the heart; they proposed things that we all want to do; but the question is, Who is going to do them? Through whose instrumentality? Are Americans ready to ask the trusts to give us in pity what we ought, in justice, to take? . . .

Shall we try to get the grip of monopoly away from our lives, or shall we not? Shall we withhold our hand and say monopoly is inevitable, that all that we can do is to regulate it? Shall we say that all that we can do is to put government in competition with monopoly and try its strength against it? Shall we admit that the creature of our own hands is stronger than we are? We have been dreading all along the time when the combined power of high finance would be greater than the power of the government. Have we come to a time when the President of the United States or any man who wishes to be the President must doff his cap in the presence of this high finance, and say, "You are our inevitable master, but we will see how we can make the best of it?"

We are at the parting of the ways. We have, not one or two or three, but many, established and formidable monopolies in the United States. We have, not one or two, but many, fields of endeavor into which it is difficult, if not impossible, for the independent man to enter. We have restricted credit, we have restricted opportunity, we have controlled development, and we have come to be one of the worst ruled, one of the most completely controlled and dominated, governments in the civilized world—no longer a government by free opinion, no longer a government by conviction and the vote of the majority, but a government by the opinion and the duress of small groups of dominant men.

If the government is to tell big business men how to run their business, then don't you see that big business men have to get closer to the government even than they are now? Don't you see that they must capture the government, in order not to be restrained too much by it? Must capture the government? They have already captured it. Are you going to invite those inside to stay inside? They don't have to get there. They are there. Are you going to own your own premises, or are you not? That is your choice. Are you going to say: "You didn't get into the house the right way, but you are in there, God bless you; we will stand out here in the cold and you can hand us out something once in a while?"

At the least, under the plan I am opposing, there will be an avowed partnership between the government and the trusts. I take it that the firm will be ostensibly controlled by the senior member. For I take it that the government of the United States is at least the senior member, though the younger member has all along been running the business. But when all the momentum, when all the energy, when a great deal of the genius, as so often happens in partnerships the world over, is with the junior partner, I don't think that the superintendence of the senior partner is going to amount to very much. And I don't believe that benevolence can be read into the hearts of the trusts by the superintendence and suggestions of the federal government; because the government has never within my recollection had its suggestions accepted by the trusts. On the contrary, the suggestions of the trusts have been accepted by the government.

There is no hope to be seen for the people of the United States until the partnership is dissolved. And the business of the party now entrusted with power is going to be to dissolve it. . . .

The Roosevelt plan is that there shall be an industrial commission charged with the supervision of the great monopolistic combinations which have been formed under the protection of the tariff, and that the government of the United States shall see to it that these gentlemen who have conquered labor shall be kind to labor. I find, then, the proposition to be this: That there shall be two masters, the great corporation, and over it the government of the United States; and I ask who is going to be master of the government of the United States? It has a master now,—those who in combination control these monopolies. And if the government controlled by the monopolies in its turn controls the monopolies, the partnership is finally consummated.

I don't care how benevolent the master is going to be, I will not live under a master. That is not what America was created for. America was created in order that every man should have the same chance as every other man to exercise mastery over his own fortunes. What I want to do is analogous to what the authorities of the city of Glasgow did with tenement houses. I want to light and patrol the corridors of these great organizations in order to see that nobody who tries to traverse them is waylaid and maltreated. If you will but hold off the adversaries, if you will but see to it that the weak are protected, I will venture a wager with you that there are some men in the United States, now weak, economically weak, who have brains enough to compete with these gentlemen and who will presently come into the market and put these gentlemen on their mettle. And the minute they come into the market there will be a bigger market for labor and a different wage scale for labor. . . .

Walter Lippmann Analyzes
The Anti-Trust Ideal
1914

The young Walter Lippmann was among those who, along with Theodore Roosevelt and Herbert Croly, felt that the way of the future was the way of large-scale organization and expert administration, not of random competition and trust-busting. In his brilliant early book, Drift and Mastery, *he stigmatized the ideals of enterprise expressed in politics by men like Bryan and Wilson (Doc. 35) as those of "a nation of villagers," and argued for a policy of mastery over the twentieth-century techniques of science and organization. Walter Lippmann,* Drift and Mastery *(New York, 1914), pp. 124-46. Also available in the Spectrum Classics in History Series.*

If the anti-trust people really grasped the full meaning of what they said, and if they really had the power or the courage to do what they proposed, they would be engaged in one of the most destructive agitations that America has known. They would be breaking up the beginning of a collective organization, thwarting the possibility of coöperation, and insisting upon submitting industry to the wasteful, the planless scramble of little profiteers. They would make impossible any deliberate and constructive use of our natural resources, they would thwart any effort to form the great industries into coördinated services, they would preserve commercialism as the undisputed master of our lives, they would lay a premium on the strategy of industrial war,—they would, if they could. For these anti-trust people have never seen the possibilities of organized industries. They have seen only the obvious evils, the birth-pains, the undisciplined strut of youth, the bad manners, the greed, and the trickery. The trusts have been ruthless, of course. No one tried to guide them; they have broken the law in a thousand ways, largely because the law was such that they had to.

At any rate, I should not like to answer before a just tribunal for the harm done this country in the last twenty-five years by the stupid hostility of anti-trust laws. How much they have perverted the constructive genius of this country it is impossible to estimate. They have blocked any policy of welcome and use, they have concentrated a nation's thinking on inessentials, they have driven creative business men to underhand methods, and put a high money value on intrigue and legal cunning, demagoguery and waste. The trusts have survived it all, but in mutilated form, the battered makeshifts of a trampled promise. They have learned every art of evasion—the only art reformers allowed them to learn.

It is said that the economy of trusts is unreal. Yet no one has ever tried the economies of the trust in any open, deliberate fashion. The amount of energy that has had to go into repelling stupid attack, the adjustments that had to be made underground—it is a wonder the trusts achieved what they did to bring order out of chaos, and forge an instrument for a nation's business. You have no more right to judge the trusts by what they are than to judge the labor movement by what it is. Both of them are in that preliminary state where they are fighting for existence, and any real outburst of constructive effort has been impossible for them.

But revolutions are not stopped by blind resistance. They are only perverted. And as an exhibition of blind resistance to a great promise, the trust campaign of the American democracy is surely unequalled. Think of contriving correctives for a revolution, such as ordering business men to compete with each other. It is as if we said: "Let not thy right hand know what thy left hand doeth; let thy right hand fight thy left hand, and in the name of God let neither win." Bernard Shaw remarked several years ago that "after all, America is not submitting to the Trusts without a struggle. The first steps have already been taken by the village constable. He is no doubt preparing a new question for immigrants" . . . after asking them whether they are anarchists or polygamists, he is to add " 'Do you approve of Trusts?' but pending this supreme measure of national defense he has declared in several states that trusts will certainly be put in the stocks and whipped."

There has been no American policy on the trust question: there has been merely a widespread resentment. The small local competitors who were wiped out became little centers of bad feeling: these nationally organized industries were looked upon as foreign invaders. They were arrogant, as the English in Ireland or the Germans in Alsace, and much of the feeling for local democracy attached itself to the revolt against these national despotisms. The trusts made enemies right and left: they squeezed the profits of the farmer, they made life difficult for the shopkeeper, they abolished jobbers and travelling salesmen, they closed down factories, they exercised an enormous control over credit through their size and through their eastern connections. Labor was no match for them, state legislatures were impotent before them. They came into the life of the simple American community as a tremendous revolutionary force, upsetting custom, changing men's status, demanding a readjustment for which people were unready. Of course, there was anti-trust feeling; of course, there was a blind desire to smash them. Men had been ruined and they were too angry to think, too hard pressed to care much about the larger life which the trusts suggested.

This feeling came to a head in Bryan's famous "cross of gold" speech in 1896. "When you come before us and tell us that we shall disturb your business interests, we reply that you have disturbed our business interests by your action. . . . The man who is employed for wages is as much a business man as his employers. The attorney in a country town is as much a business man as the corporation counsel in a great metropolis. The merchant at the crossroads store is as much a business man as the merchant of New York. The farmer . . . is as much a business man as the man who goes upon the Board of Trade and bets upon the price of grain. The miners . . . It is for these that we speak . . . we are fighting in the defense of our homes, our families, and posterity." What Bryan was really defending was the old and simple life of America, a life that was doomed by the great organization that had come into the world. He thought he was fighting the plutocracy: as a matter of fact he was fighting something much deeper than that; he was fighting the larger scale of human life. The Eastern money power controlled the new industrial system, and Bryan fought it. But what he and his people hated from the bottom of their souls were the economic conditions which had upset the old life of the prairies, made new demands upon democracy, introduced specialization and science, had destroyed village loyalties, frustrated private ambitions, and created the impersonal relationships of the modern world.

Bryan has never been able to adjust himself to the new world in which he lives. That is why he is so irresistibly funny to sophisticated newspapermen. His virtues, his habits, his ideas, are the simple, direct, shrewd qualities of early America. He is the true Don Quixote of our politics, for he moves in a world that has ceased to exist.

He is a more genuine conservative than some propertied bigot. Bryan stands for the popular tradition of America, whereas most of his enemies stand merely for the power that is destroying that tradition. Bryan is what America was; his critics are generally defenders of what America has become. And neither seems to have any vision of what America is to be.

Yet there has always been great power behind Bryan, the power of those who in one way or another were hurt by the greater organization that America was developing. The Populists were part of that power. La Follette and the insurgent Republicans expressed it. It was easily a political majority of the American people. The Republican Party disintegrated under the pressure of the revolt. The Bull Moose gathered much of its strength from it. The Socialists have got some of it. But in 1912 it swept the Democratic Party, and by a combination of circumstances, carried the country. The plutocracy was beaten in politics, and the power that Bryan spoke for in 1896, the forces that had made muckraking popular, captured the government. They were led by a man who was no part of the power that he represented.

Woodrow Wilson is an outsider capable of skilled interpretation. He is an historian, and that has helped him to know the older tradition of America. He is a student of theory, and like most theorists of his generation he is deeply attached to the doctrines that swayed the world when America was founded.

But Woodrow Wilson at least knows that there is a new world. "There is one great basic fact which underlies all the questions that are discussed on the political platform at the present moment. That singular fact is that nothing is done in this country as it was done twenty years ago. We are in the presence of a new organization of society. . . . We have changed our economic conditions, absolutely, from top to bottom; and, with our economic society, the organization of our life." You could not make a more sweeping statement of the case. The President is perfectly aware of what has happened, and he says at the very outset that "our laws still deal with us on the basis of the old system . . . the old positive formulas do not fit the present problems."

You wait eagerly for some new formula. The new formula is this: "I believe the time has come when the governments of this country, both state and national, have to set the stage, and set it very minutely and carefully, for the doing of justice to men in every relationship of life." Now that is a new formula, because it means a willingness to use the power of government much more extensively.

But for what purpose is this power to be used? There, of course, is the rub. It is to be used to "*restore* our politics to their full spiritual vigor *again,* and our national life, whether in trade, in industry, or in what concerns us only as families and individuals, to its purity, its self-respect, and its *pristine* strength and freedom." The ideal is the old ideal, the ideal of Bryan, the method is the new one of government interference.

That, I believe, is the inner contradiction of Woodrow Wilson. He knows that there is a new world demanding new methods, but he dreams of an older world. He is torn between the two. It is a very deep conflict in him between what he knows and what he feels.

His feeling is, as he says, for "the man on the make." "For my part,

I want the pigmy to have a chance to come out" . . . "Just let some o.
the youngsters I know have a chance and they'll give these gentlemer
points. Lend them a little money. They can't get any now. See to it tha
when they have got a local market they can't be squeezed out of it.'
Nowhere in his speeches will you find any sense that it may be possible
to organize the fundamental industries on some deliberate plan for na
tional service. He is thinking always about somebody's chance to buile
up a profitable business; he likes the idea that somebody can beat some
body else, and the small business man takes on the virtues of David in
a battle with Goliath.

"Have you found trusts that thought as much of their men as they
did of their machinery?" he asks, forgetting that few people have ever
found competitive textile mills or clothing factories that did. There isn'
an evil of commercialism that Wilson isn't ready to lay at the door o
the trusts. He becomes quite reckless in his denunciation of the New
Devil—Monopoly—and of course, by contrast the competitive busines
takes on a halo of light. It is amazing how clearly he sees the evils tha
trusts do, how blind he is to the evils that his supporters do. You woule
think that the trusts were the first oppressors of labor; you would thinl
they were the first business organization that failed to achieve the highes
possible efficiency. The pretty record of competition throughout the Nine
teenth Century is forgotten. Suddenly all that is a glorious past which
we have lost. You would think that competitive commercialism wa
really a generous, chivalrous, high-minded stage of human culture.

"We design that the limitations on private enterprise shall be removed
so that the next generation of youngsters, as they come along, will no
have to become protégés of benevolent trusts, but will be free to go
about making their own lives what they will; so that we shall taste agair
the full cup, not of charity, but of liberty,—the only wine that ever re
freshed and renewed the spirit of a people." That cup of liberty—we
may well ask him to go back to Manchester, to Paterson to-day, to the
garment trades of New York, and taste it for himself.

The New Freedom means the effort of small business men and farmer
to use the government against the larger collective organization of in
dustry. Wilson's power comes from them; his feeling is with them; his
thinking is for them. Never a word of understanding for the new type
of administrator, the specialist, the professionally trained business man
practically no mention of the consumer—even the tariff is for the busi
ness man; no understanding of the new demands of labor, its solidarity
its aspiration for some control over the management of business; no hint
that it may be necessary to organize the fundamental industries of the

country on some definite plan so that our resources may be developed by scientific method instead of by men "on the make"; no friendliness for the larger, collective life upon which the world is entering, only a constant return to the commercial chances of young men trying to set up in business. That is the push and force of this New Freedom, a freedom for the little profiteer, but no freedom for the nation from the narrowness, the poor incentives, the limited vision of small competitors,—no freedom from clamorous advertisement, from wasteful selling, from duplication of plants, from unnecessary enterprise, from the chaos, the welter, the strategy of industrial war.

There is no doubt, I think, that President Wilson and his party represent primarily small business in a war against the great interests. Socialists speak of his administration as a revolution within the bounds of capitalism. Wilson doesn't really fight the oppressions of property. He fights the evil done by large property-holders to small ones. The temper of his administration was revealed very clearly when the proposal was made to establish a Federal Trade Commission. It was suggested at once by leading spokesmen of the Democratic Party that corporations with a capital of less than a million dollars should be exempted from supervision. Is that because little corporations exploit labor or the consumer less? Not a bit of it. It is because little corporations are in control of the political situation.

But there are certain obstacles to the working out of the New Freedom. First of all, there was a suspicion in Wilson's mind, even during the campaign, that the tendency to large organization was too powerful to be stopped by legislation. So he left open a way of escape from the literal achievement of what the New Freedom seemed to threaten. *"I am for big business,"* he said, *"and I am against the trusts."* That is a very subtle distinction, so subtle, I suspect, that no human legislation will ever be able to make it. The distinction is this: big business is a business that has survived competition; a trust is an arrangement to do away with competition. But when competition is done away with, who is the Solomon wise enough to know whether the result was accomplished by superior efficiency or by agreement among the competitors or by both?

The big trusts have undoubtedly been built up in part by superior business ability, and by successful competition, but also by ruthless competition, by underground arrangements, by an intricate series of facts which no earthly tribunal will ever be able to disentangle. And why should it try? These great combinations are here. What interests us is not their history but their future. The point is whether you are going to split them up, and if so into how many parts. Once split, are they to be kept from coming together again? Are you determined to prevent men who could coöperate from coöperating? Wilson seems to imply that a big business which has survived competition is to be let alone, and the trusts attacked. But as there is no real way of distinguishing between them, he leaves the question just where he found it: he must choose between the large organization of business and the small.

It's here that his temperament and his prejudices clash with fact and necessity. He really would like to disintegrate large business. "Are you not eager for the time," he asks, "when your sons shall be able to look forward to becoming not employees, but heads of some small, it may be, but hopeful business . . . ?" But to what percentage of the population can he hold out that hope? How many small but hopeful steel mills, coal mines, telegraph systems, oil refineries, copper mines, can this country support? A few hundred at the outside. And for these few hundred sons whose "best energies . . . are inspired by the knowledge that they are their own masters with the paths of the world before them," we are asked to give up the hope of a sane, deliberate organization of national industry brought under democratic control.

I submit that it is an unworthy dream. I submit that the intelligent men of my generation can find a better outlet for their energies than in making themselves masters of little businesses. They have the vast opportunity of introducing order and purpose into the business world, of devising administrative methods by which the great resources of the country can be operated on some thought-out plan. They have the whole new field of industrial statesmanship before them, and those who prefer the egotism of some little business are not the ones whose ambitions we need most to cultivate. . . .

Wilson is against the trusts for many reasons: the political economy of his generation was based on competition and free trade; the Democratic Party is by tradition opposed to a strong central government, and that opposition applies equally well to strong national business,—it is a party attached to local rights, to village patriotism, to humble but ambitious enterprise; its temper has always been hostile to specialization and expert knowledge, because it admires a very primitive man-to-man democracy. Wilson's thought is inspired by that outlook. It has been tempered somewhat by contact with men who have outgrown the village culture, so that Wilson is less hostile to experts, less oblivious to administrative problems than is Bryan. But at the same time his speeches are marked with contempt for the specialist: they play up quite obviously to the old democratic notion that any man can do almost any job. . . .

Hostility to large organization is a natural quality in village life. Wilson is always repeating that the old personal relationships of employer and employee have disappeared. He deplores the impersonal nature of the modern world. Now that is a fact not to be passed over lightly. It does change the nature of our problems enormously. Indeed, it is just this breakdown of the old relationships which constitutes the modern problem. . . . There is a growing body of opinion which says that communication is blotting out village culture, and opening up national and international thought. It says that bad as big business is to-day, it has a wide promise within it, and that the real task of our generation is to realize it. It looks to the infusion of scientific method, the careful application of administrative technique, the organization and education of the consumer for control, the discipline of labor for an increasing share of the management. Those of us who hold such a belief are pushed from behind by what we think is an irresistible economic development, and lured by a future which we think is possible.

We don't imagine that the trusts are going to drift naturally into the service of human life. We think they can be made to serve it if the American people compel them. We think that the American people may be able to do that if they can adjust their thinking to a new world situation, if they apply the scientific spirit to daily life, and if they can learn to coöperate on a large scale. Those, to be sure, are staggering *ifs*. The conditions may never be fulfilled entirely. But in so far as they are not fulfilled we shall drift along at the mercy of economic forces that we are unable to master. Those who cling to the village view of life may deflect the drift, may batter the trusts about a bit, but they will never dominate business, never humanize its machinery, and they will continue to be the playthings of industrial change.

Eyewitness Accounts of American History

This series provides the reader with an immediate sense of how the American people lived and thought in the pivotal periods of our history. In each volume, a leading historian has assembled and annotated first-hand reports, personal accounts, and statements of influential spokesmen of the time.

70
71
72
74
75
76
77
79
83
88